Time Alive

Time Alive

CELEBRATE YOUR LIFE EVERY DAY

ALEXANDRA STODDARD

Collins

An Imprint of HarperCollinsPublishers

To Peter with love

❀

HarperCollins books may be purchased for educational, business, or sales
promotional use. For information, please write: Special Markets Department,
HarperCollins Publishers Inc., 10 East 53rd Street, New York, NY 10022.

FIRST EDITION

p.27 from *Time and the Art of Living* by Robert Grudin, copyright © 1982
by Robert Grudin. Reprinted by permission of HarperCollins Publishers Inc.

Designed by Lorie Pagnozzi

Printed on acid-free paper

Library of Congress Cataloging-in-Publication Data is available upon request.

ISBN-10: 0-06-079664-2
ISBN-13: 978-0-06-079664-8

05 06 07 08 09 ❖/RDD 10 9 8 7 6 5 4 3 2

I sincerely acknowledge with admiration and deep
appreciation my literary agent, Carl Brandt; my editor,
Toni Sciarra; and my assistant, Sharon Scarpa; as well as my
family, friends, and readers who have encouraged and
inspired me during my writing of this book.

❋

Real life is found only in the present. If people tell you that you should
live your life preparing for the future, do not believe them. We live in this life,
and we know this life only, and therefore all our efforts should be directed
toward the improvement of this life. Not your life in general, but every
hour of this life should be lived in the best way you know how.

—LEO TOLSTOY

❋

Contents

CHAPTER FOUR: *Enthusiasm*

CHAPTER FIVE: *Caring*

CHAPTER SIX: *Purpose*

CHAPTER SEVEN: *Spirit*

This book is all about time. I've written many books about different aspects of life, ranging from design, beauty and color, to mothering, love and happiness. Since the mid-seventies I've wanted to write a book about how to use time wisely. In these thirty years I've had lots of time to think. I believe if we can figure out how to put time to wise use, we've unlocked the door that holds a secret to every part of our lives. Nothing happens outside of time. Our entire life is experienced within the movement of time.

All we have is time, and we must become wise with our time. I am at peace with time. Many people are not. The only time we are alive is now. If there is something we want to do in our lifetime, we should begin it now. When we put time to constructive use, we'll feel fully alive, intensely engaged in living, at peace with the fact our life won't last forever. When we value time as our greatest prize, we become extremely selective about how we allocate our precious moments. Now we can stop taking our time for granted.

I've learned how to stretch time. I do what has to be done in the spirit of opportunity and challenge. I now realistically accept the vast amounts of time that I spend on necessary aspects of my life while trying to keep everything in a healthy balance. I regularly make time for what I believe is important to me, savoring *being*, not always feeling I have to be *doing* something. In this book I hope to show there are several hours a day that we can seize and claim as our own free time. We need to take stock, and rethink everything. We need to make the connection between how we spend our time and how well we live our lives.

I wrote this book as a wakeup call, to remind us that now is the only time there is. The good news is that we all can learn intelligently to save, make, spend and enjoy all of our time alive. My book teaches skills and ideas you can develop to change the way you approach every aspect of your given time and your own life. All time is to be cherished and savored. We can learn to spend time well in rapid-fire mini-seconds, as well as elevate moments to timeless, memorable little private epiphanies.

Life is only time. We have this gift allotted to us while we're alive. Choose well what you do with the time you're given. You will live a good life as a result. Time is depleting, whether you pay attention or not. My dearest wish for you is that you find this vital message of value and that you celebrate *your time alive every day*.

LOVE,

Alexandra Stoddard

CHAPTER ONE

Time

Now Is the Only Time We Have to Live Fully and Well

FOR ETERNALLY AND ALWAYS THERE IS ONLY NOW, ONE AND THE SAME NOW; THE PRESENT IS THE ONLY THING THAT HAS NO END.

ALAN WATTS

Our time alive is brief by any standard. Now is the only opportunity we'll have to give our life meaning and find satisfaction in our daily lives. We will not be given a second chance.

Each of us is given an unknown amount of time alive on this planet. While we are alive we live from one moment to the next. The seconds become minutes. Sixty minutes become an hour. The time to be all that you dream of becoming is now—right now, right here where you are. It is said that the ancient Greeks whispered to each other every morning, "If not now, when?"

We have no guarantees or certainties; the only certainty we have is this present alive moment, this precious gift of time. When we breathe deeply in this specific point in time; when we stay focused and really pay attention, we give our lives significance. Our big moment is now. Our moment of truth is now. Our entire life depends on our wise use of our moments.

We put our time alive to good and proper use minute to minute, moment to moment, in the course of our waking time, or we lose it forever. Now is here, not there. We are alive only now, not then.

When we bring ourselves into each moment fully, intensely, enthusiastically, we're awake to the magnitude of our lives. Time can't be revisited, changed or improved. The only time that we're able to think and act intelligently, to fulfill what we believe is most important, is in our time alive now.

When we begin to live from point to point, we fill in the dots of time beautifully and well. When we concentrate fully on now, we become enlightened. The air is more clear, the sky is more blue, the light is so brilliant it dazzles our imaginations. We can experience the big picture of our lives in our present consciousness. We see the acorn and envision a forest of oak trees. We understand that the baby we are holding in our arms will one day be a grown mother who will hold her baby in her arms. The flow and continuity of our lives is all present in this moment. When we appreciate the truth about our time alive, we're able to put great value on every moment because we're able to see the great possibilities for living beautifully and feeling lasting inner happiness.

At this moment, we are making memories for a future time. We don't live now in order to be able to look back at our past; our past is moved forward into our present time alive through the blessings of our memory. Our now moments encompass our past and resonate in our unknown future. Our beginning, middle and end are enclosed in a circle of *now awareness*.

When we purify our thoughts in this moment, we are free from our past and are able to let go of anything that has been holding us back. We're here now. The only window of time we have to love our life, love ourselves and love others, is when we're alive. We're able now to touch, to taste, to smell, to hear and to see all of the wonders around us. We're alive to the tenderness, the kindness, and the love that is inside us and everywhere. We're truly alive and all is well.

The past is no longer alive. The future has not been born. Living well now is creating eternity. Our future entirely depends on this present real-life moment. When we live fully and well now, our time alive is sacred.

❋

A MAN MUST HAVE A SHARE IN THE PASSIONS AND
ACTIONS OF HIS TIME, AT THE PERIL OF BEING JUDGED
NOT TO HAVE LIVED.

JUSTICE OLIVER WENDELL HOLMES

Live Each Day as Your First and Your Last

LET OTHERS WORSHIP THE PAST; I MUCH PREFER THE PRESENT,
AM DELIGHTED TO BE ALIVE TODAY.
OVID

*I*f you could live your life backward, what would you do differently? What would you not have done? What would you do that you didn't do? Ask yourself these questions briefly before you completely focus on today.

Two thousand five hundred years ago Plato pondered the concept of the reversal of time. Visualize going backward in your life, when you were looking forward to events such as graduation, marriage or the birth of a child. In every chapter of our lives, we should live with as few regrets as possible. Do this exercise once, but don't dwell on your past, because it cannot be changed.

Time doesn't reverse; it moves us forward in the clockwise direction of life's currents and never stops moving us along in the stream of life's exhilarating challenges and miraculous experiences, as well as loss. Nothing alive ever stays the same.

Many great thinkers throughout history have urged us to live each day with vitality and vigor, as though it were the last day of our time alive. If it were our last day, what would our thoughts be? Who would we want to share these moments with? Where would we choose to be? In reality, a day is a miniature lifetime, from sunrise to sunset. We're alive to this great event—today.

When we live as though today, this precious day, were our first as well as our last, we see everything with greater love and appreciation. With childlike wonder we lose all sense of time, and when we are out of time, we are out of body. We connect to life with great excitement. Today is our time alive to spend however we choose. We have our morning hours, our midday, our afternoon, and our evening. Each sixty-minute hour lived well is a celebration of our time alive. Each hour provides us ample time to be productive, to feel compassion, to be gentle and kind to ourselves and those with whom we share our lives.

How do you choose to live today? How do you intend to spend and use your twenty-four hours? How can you experience the most meaningful day of your life up until now? Each morning when I wake up, I breathe in and say under my breath, "Time alive." I've been given today. I have been given time to live, to love, to celebrate, to learn, to grow, to be excited and to be happy.

Living today as though it were our first and our last awakens us to a greater sense of reverence for life, a deeper sense of wonder and awe. We feel joyful, hopeful, young and fresh. Our vital energy and our creative powers are keen. When we hold the view that this might be the last time we hold our loved one in our arms, or the last time we are able to dance or unite physically, the present becomes so expansive, so poignant, so magnificent, we feel complete, whole and connected to the great mystery of life. We are given an example of what our entire life can be like. We have a standard to follow.

Take some time to think of all the people in your life whom you love. Hold them up in your consciousness. As a useful exercise, envision them no longer alive. Consider your not being alive. Live this day with that awareness and your day will be a triumphant celebration of lasting significance.

There is no time to think small. Think big, expansive thoughts about your life and what you want to leave behind. Today is not an ordinary day. Today is rich with blessings and sweet with radiant love. Today is the first day of the rest of your time alive.

✻

BEGIN AT ONCE TO LIVE, AND COUNT EACH SEPARATE DAY
AS A SEPARATE LIFE.

SENECA

※ 3 ※

Experience Time Alive Moments

I TRY TO STAY CONSCIOUS OF EVERY MOMENT.

OPRAH WINFREY

*W*hen we focus our energies fully in the moment, with an athlete's sense of single-minded concentration, we experience what I call "time alive moments." Light enters our consciousness. Aha! Our mindset has expanded. We see and know something new. We have an insight into truth that we didn't have before.

Here you are consciously awake to all that is happening around you and inside you. You, as if suddenly, experience the intensity of being alive, of your being an integral part of creation. You become more intimately aware of your relationship to the universe. You feel your wholeness, your deep love of this life. You awaken to the fact that this present moment could be the best of your entire life.

When did you last have a time alive moment? They are dramatic in their intensity, as though we were awakened for the first time.

I remember once sitting down to write a love letter to a man who was in his final days alive. He was ninety-three years old and had stopped eating. He was skin and bones, ready to go to his eternal home. I sat silently, meditating on how much I loved this man. Bob O'Brien's genius recognized my longings when I began to write forty years ago; he became my teacher and literary mentor.

I sat still, hands outstretched on the cool marble-topped table, tears flowing, as I said good-bye. So often we don't appreciate what we have until it is taken away from us, but not a day goes by without my gratitude for all Bob has taught me, all the wisdom he freely gave when I was young and starting out.

Time alive moments come when we're most aware of all the gifts that have been given us, of all the people we are united with. These moments come when we are still and receptive to transformation of conscious awareness.

In writing my letter I captured the feeling of timelessness—in the late sixties, Bob and I played mixed doubles tennis together. My mind and heart recalled when he cut in on me at a dance and asked me what I was writing—he'd seen me sitting under a tree at the tennis club, writing in spiral notebooks between tennis matches.

Time alive moments are independent; they're eternal and unaffected by time. We get into a trance—an ecstatic state where our sharp concentration evolves into contemplation, and we daydream. We become, for a moment, detached from our physical surroundings and visualize other worlds, other events. Best not to have a time alive moment when you're driving a car!

The greatest gift of these time alive moments is the freedom we feel from commotion or disturbance, anxiety or tension. We are not restless. We become tranquil, calm, steady and serene. We've expanded our horizons. We've connected ourselves to our most intimate personal understanding of who we are.

In time alive moments is eternity. In a moment, we can and often do experience timelessness. I remember when my daughter Alexandra's third child was born and I held Lily in my arms. When she looked into my eyes, her eye contact was so complete. I felt we had been together forever.

Timeless moments, time alive moments, can spontaneously happen when someone we love unites in intimate eye contact and smiles at us, or when watching a sunrise or sunset, walking on a deserted beach, stargazing, or when we arrange flowers or garden or paint. When we read great poetry, we sense the timelessness of each meaningful experience. The quality of these mysterious, mystical moments depends on the preparedness of our mind, heart, body and spirit. Recognizing magical moments, sublime moments, time alive moments, transforms us, transports us, and lets us transcend to infinite potential and vast possibilities for our life's journey.

❀

'WE DO NOT REMEMBER DAYS, WE REMEMBER MOMENTS.

CESARE PAVESE

Timing Is Crucial

TIMING IS EVERYTHING.

ALEXANDRA B. STODDARD

*T*he most productive, creative thinkers and most content people tend to have an innate sense of timing. It is up to us to discover what this divine, ideal timing is, and to act accordingly.

There has to be synchronization, a regulation of all factors and the consequences of the action. This is true in music, in the theater, in athletics and in our normal daily life. There is a coming together in one place, at one time, in balance and with a sense of urgency. We need to pace ourselves to create the right timing. We need to schedule and coordinate our actions in order to achieve a desired result.

Any imbalance, action delayed or premature, throws the timing off. As a former tennis player, I learned to throw the ball up high and in front of me when serving, so I could hit the ball at precisely the moment before it descended. The more I practiced, the more prepared I was to hit the ball at the correct time, the more often I would win my serve.

There are good times and bad times to do and say things. If we're going to have a serious talk with our spouse, we should pick a time and place where we're going to have privacy, where we'll have no interruptions and when we are in a loving, empathetic mood. The point of the conversation is to be heard and understood. Our innate sense of the best timing will infuse the atmosphere with understanding and thoughtfulness.

When our children are young, before they go off to school, we know it is wise to spend time with them at home. Timing is everything in these critical, early developing years.

When Peter and I travel between our New York City apartment and our cottage in Connecticut, we often change our plans by a day or two in order to complete some projects and not feel scattered. We travel by train, so we're conscious of the traffic patterns getting to the station and back, and try to go at a time when the train won't be too crowded. We often leave on a Saturday morning to avoid the trucks and congestion.

We learn when it is most productive for us to do creative work. If you are freshest in the morning, even if you have young children at home, you can go to bed earlier and get up before your children do so that you'll have some silence and time to think, fresh from a good night's sleep. If you're planning to go on an island vacation, you won't arrange your trip during the rainy, hurricane season if you have a choice. With planning and preparation, and a desire to have your life run as smoothly as possible, respect timing's wisdom and plan according to the best of your ability. When you face some difficulties, don't give up too soon. You'll lose everything. Often, difficult times are opportunities to use our strength to find solutions. Proper respect for time can guide you into doing the right thing, at the right time, for the right reason.

✻

WE CANNOT MAKE IT RAIN, BUT WE CAN SEE TO IT THAT
THE RAIN FALLS ON PREPARED SOIL.

HENRI J. M. NOUWEN

Be in the Swing of Time

CREATIVE PEOPLE ARE ALL THERE, TOTALLY IMMERSED, FASCINATED
AND ABSORBED IN THE PRESENT, IN THE CURRENT SITUATION, IN THE
HERE-NOW, WITH THE MATTER-IN-HAND.

ABRAHAM MASLOW

*W*hen we're fully alive, intensely excited about the task at hand, we feel the exhilaration of our vitality. We're focused, as if swimming with the tide. The wind is at our back and we feel as though we're being pushed by some invisible force. We move forward as if suspended from above. We move with ease, breathe deeply, smile easily. In the swing of time, we skip and literally jump with joy.

Fortunately, we can train ourselves to be in the swing of time. We must be prepared in order to activate this elevated mood: we need to be present-mindful, we need to stay in this flow state, we need to allow ourselves ample time to do a task or complete an experience without rushing. When we hurry, we snuff out the pleasure of whatever we are doing; we become anxious, frustrated and lose our awareness of the moment we are living. We make mistakes because we aren't able to think clearly.

Hurry-scurry causes confusion. We don't have the full force of our five senses. Speeding up the process with undue haste can be and often is extremely dangerous. Jumping a traffic light is shortsighted. A woman who worked in an eyeglass shop in Michigan was paid in ten parts of an hour on the time clock. If she was late, she'd lose the entire hour's pay. One morning she overslept and rushing to work she got into an automobile accident, lost four days of work, and did two thousand dollars' worth of uninsured damage to her car.

When a college student came home for a vacation, he was singing in the shower, washing his hair, thoroughly enjoying himself. In between song notes he heard the telephone ring. He rushed to answer it, slipped on the marble floor, skidded into the bedroom and broke a window with his elbow. What is the lesson to learn from this unnecessary accident? When taking a shower, enjoy the shower. After you've finished and dressed, check your phone machine for a message.

Suppose when you leave the house in a rush, you forget your grocery list. Being distracted by trying to remember what to buy, you lock your keys in the car with your baby still in his car seat. Have you ever left your credit card at a restaurant because you left without thinking?

Some people have a habit of rushing even when they have no place to go. This sense of urgent hurrying is graceless, frantic and a poor use of your time alive. There is a rhythm to life. Being in the swing of time completes each experience in a satisfactory and satisfying way. We must take time to enjoy this swing state. There is a great exhilaration in being in touch with the process of our lives. We're more alive when we're aware of the series of actions we take as we do myriad things throughout the day.

When we're in the swing, we're able to train our mind to think more clearly, become more aware and more vitally alive. Every chore, each grace note, every pleasant or necessary activity, will have more meaning, be more fun, and be more lively when we're in the swing, in sync with time.

❀

MIRACLES, IN THE SENSE OF PHENOMENA WE CANNOT EXPLAIN,
SURROUND US ON EVERY HAND:
LIFE ITSELF IS THE MIRACLE OF MIRACLES.

GEORGE BERNARD SHAW

What You Don't Do Is Often More Important Than What You Do

IT TAKES COURAGE TO DO WHAT *YOU* WANT. OTHER PEOPLE HAVE A LOT OF PLANS FOR YOU. NOBODY WANTS YOU TO DO WHAT YOU WANT TO DO. THEY WANT YOU TO GO ON THEIR TRIP. BUT YOU CAN DO WHAT YOU WANT. I DID. I WENT TO THE WOODS AND READ FOR FIVE YEARS.

JOSEPH CAMPBELL

*A*n exceedingly accomplished artist and designer asked me over a long, leisurely lunch once, "Alexandra, how do you find time to do all you do?" I laughed. "Adrian, it is what I choose not to do that frees me up to do all I wish to do. I have the freedom to decide what I want to do and how I decide to spend my time."

We're either a slave to time, or time becomes our servant. I am the only person alive who can control how I live my life. I have always carefully guarded my time. Ever since I was a little girl, I've always had things I've wanted to do that make me happy, things that I feel are good for me and good for others. I never wait around to see what others have in mind for me.

I was giving a talk at the Ritz-Carlton in Chicago several years ago and my very dear friend Wendy was there. During interaction after my lecture, Wendy raised her hand to share an insight with the audience. Everyone was remembering their childhood and what characteristics we share with our mothers. Wendy remembered that every time she'd come over to play with me, my mother put her to work. It didn't matter what my mother was doing, Wendy was urged to join in. She ended up along with me washing the car, watering the roses, or husking corn.

Because of my mother's strong personality, I learned early on to go to Wendy's house so we could play, not work. When I wasn't escaping the house to play with a friend, I'd go to the public tennis courts at the nearby high school and hit balls against a backboard or practice my serve with the bag of balls the pro would loan me. Occasionally, old Doc Marshall would come onto the court and rally with me. He'd take a dime out of his baggy sharkskin shorts and place it where he wanted me to aim my serve or my cross-court backhand. By playing tennis, I avoided doing grown-ups' chores that I chose not to get trapped into doing.

On Friday nights I am struck by the great joy I feel being able to work right up until eight o'clock, when Peter and I head out to dinner. Ever since I've been earning a living I've always loved the "carrot" theory of having something pleasurable to look forward to after doing something productive. My favorite evening to go out for dinner is Friday night. It is the end of a workweek, the beginning of the weekend and a romantic time to wear something colorful and have a date with my husband, Peter—whom I refer to as my boyfriend.

The bliss lies in the unfolding afternoon hours when I don't have to concern myself about buying and preparing dinner. I can sit outside in our tiny garden on a small brick terrace and be surrounded by flowers. While I write, there are no house guests, no expectations from others. I am free in every sense of the word.

There are a great many things I could do to occupy my time, but I've established time boundaries by eliminating certain things from my daily life that would fill up my time. When Peter and I are at the cottage, we've learned how to thrive by giving up modern conveniences: we have a television set, but don't have cable, so we occasionally watch an old classic movie as if we were having a night out at the theater. We have a microwave oven that we use to store our tea in; I've never used it for cooking. We had the plumber disconnect our dishwasher and ice machine because of frozen pipes and condensation damage. I use the dishwasher as a drain board and make ice cubes in a plastic tray. We have no washing machine or dryer because in an eighteenth-century house like ours, the best place for that modern equipment would be in the basement; I'm not interested in spending time in a dreary old underground space. We have no computer or printer and, therefore, we don't use email—much to my friends' horror.

We have no air conditioner; we use overhead fans and countertop ones that oscillate. We have no car; we ride our bikes, take trains and taxis to get around.

If I had a large family with young children at home, I would have to readjust my priorities, but my child-rearing days are behind me. We usually go to visit our grandchildren in their home, where they're able to adhere to their schedule and be happy with their familiar things.

By keeping everything simple and straightforward, I feel I'm able to free up my time. Most everyone who knows me tries to get me to use a computer to write my books. (I'm given free advice about computers and other "time-savers"quite regularly.) But I'm at a place in my life where I feel comfortable with myself, keeping in mind my limitations and my priorities. I continuously try to find ways to stay in touch and in tune with the rhythms of time, finding pleasure in the most quotidian domestic tasks.

Not hearing the noise from the dishwasher and the *plunk*, *plunk*, *plunk* of the ice machine's cubes dropping allows me the luxury of listening to the birds singing to me as I enjoy quiet time at the kitchen table without distractions or interruptions. I enjoy writing letters in this nice atmosphere as well as reading and writing ideas in a notebook. I feel so cozy and the silence inspires my muse.

We all have to establish time boundaries and learn how to say no. When we understand just how precious our time alive really is, we begin to carve out our particular patterns for our individual lives. We're better able to determine our priorities and to stick to them. We learn to see, feel, and know the best way to spend our most valuable resource—our time.

Saying no is central to freeing up time and space in order to live well. Carry the tool of *no* with you wherever your life leads you. All wise people create strict time boundaries in order to create an atmosphere where they can thrive.

❋

IF WE DON'T TAKE CHARGE OF ITS DIRECTION, OUR LIFE WILL BE CONTROLLED BY THE OUTSIDE. HOW WE CHOOSE WHAT TO DO, AND HOW WE APPROACH IT, THAT WILL DETERMINE WHETHER THE SUM OF OUR DAYS ADDS UP TO A FORMLESS BLUR, OR TO SOMETHING RESEMBLING A WORK OF ART.

MIHALY CSIKSZENTMIHALYI

Everything Takes Longer Than You Think

HAVE PATIENCE WITH ALL THINGS, BUT CHIEFLY
HAVE PATIENCE WITH YOURSELF.

SAINT FRANCIS DE SALES

*M*ost of us are unrealistic about how long it takes to accomplish something. In order to avoid anxiety and the stress of always feeling behind, we have to establish realistic expectations for ourselves and others.

My husband, Peter Brown, came up with "Brown's Law" after observing human behavior over several decades: whenever we or others estimate how many hours of labor it will take to complete a project, we are rarely accurate because we tend to underestimate the time it will actually take.

Twenty years ago I was hired as the interior designer for a new bank building in Amarillo, Texas. In my contract I was offered a bonus if I completed the project within budget and on time. I believe in private enterprise, because it always involves personal incentive. I received the bonus—just barely.

As an interior designer, I always get a firm estimate for my clients so there won't be any surprises. While all price guesses are based on time and materials, rarely does anyone offer to give money back because the job took less time. When a contractor is paid on a time-and-material basis, the hours expand. Also, there are so often contingencies, situations that come up, uncertainties you didn't plan on.

When people decide to lose weight, they may estimate it will take three months to lose twenty pounds. They drop the first ten pounds in two weeks.

After another month, they shed five more pounds before hitting a plateau where weight is not lost or gained, but maintained. In reality, the last five pounds are lost incrementally over the next three months.

One large publishing firm took the bold step of canceling contracts with writers whose manuscripts were not submitted on time. No writer knows for certain how long it will take to write a book. We learn from the actual doing, and often we are amazed how many hours go into thinking through and writing a book.

The first few years after we planted rose bushes along our picket fence, I was unsure how to prune them after they bloomed. When I inquired of a gardener friend, I was told that each blossom needs to be cut back just above a five-leaf section for strength so that the plant will rebloom later in the summer. Our roses have grown and there are thousands of dead blossoms that need to be carefully cut off. Because they're our beautiful rose bushes, it is a pleasure to prune them, but it is no quick task.

We have to be patient with ourselves and others. Whether we're tending our roses or raising a child, when we love life and care deeply, we will be investing our time wisely. In all important matters, there are no shortcuts. When we acknowledge that what we are doing with our time is of lasting value to us and others and we believe that we are doing the right thing, taking the time needed is worth it.

I STILL FIND EVERY DAY TOO SHORT FOR ALL THE THOUGHTS
I WANT TO THINK, ALL THE WALKS I WANT TO TAKE, ALL THE BOOKS I WANT
TO READ, AND ALL THE FRIENDS I WANT TO SEE. THE LONGER I LIVE THE MORE
MY MIND DWELLS UPON THE BEAUTY AND THE WONDER OF THE WORLD.

JOHN BURROUGHS

You Have 8,766 Hours a Year to Act Wisely

HOW CAN YOU HESITATE? RISK! RISK ANYTHING! CARE NO MORE FOR
THE OPINION OF OTHERS ... DO THE HARDEST THING
ON EARTH FOR YOU. ACT FOR YOURSELF. FACE THE TRUTH.

KATHERINE MANSFIELD

So often we wish we had more hours in a day. But there's no sense complaining about time. Time is not our enemy. While in life we're not all given the same time in years, we're each given the same amount of time every hour. When we abuse the time we do have—by mismanagement or not thinking things through—do we feel our life spinning out of control?

The best way to wrap our arms around time and find several free hours each day for us to put to wise use is to break time into sixty-minute sections, looking at the hours and their portions in order to determine how we are using our time.

Everyone's life is different, but we all eat, sleep, bathe, and carry out daily rituals in similar ways. In looking in detail at our time structure, we see with greater clarity how we can free up more time for our own use. Generalizations are only a guess and only you know the reality of how and where you spend your hours.

Take a typical day. Of the twenty-four hours, how much is taken up in sleep? We generally allot eight hours for sleep, leaving us with sixteen waking hours. Be precise. Do you take an afternoon nap? Realistically write down how many waking hours you have on average. How many hours of sleep do you require to feel energetic in the morning? Obviously, if you're tired, you will not be as clearheaded when you're able to carve out some time.

Approximately half of our waking time is taken up with work. An eight-hour workday, including a lunch hour, leaves you with eight hours to take care of your daily requirements. Some people work twelve hours a day, leaving only four hours for everything else.

Take time to write down all the responsibilities you have at home. Once you identify them, determine how much time each one takes. How much time do you require for grocery shopping, meal planning, preparation, eating and cleaning up? On average, how much time do you require for bathing, exercise, car pool, beauty treatments, clothes shopping, maintaining the car, cleaning and keeping your house in fresh repair? How much time do you spend with childcare? How much time do you spend with your family? Walking the dog or going to doctors' appointments?

Write down everything you do in a day, a week, a month, and a year. Add up what you literally do—bill paying, filing, talking on the telephone, emailing, time spent on the computer, watching television, going to the movies or to dinner, going away for the weekend with the children, commuting. Identify all of your habits and time patterns. A recent survey conducted by the Department of Labor found that the average adult, working or nonworking, had more than five hours of leisure time a day and that he or she spent half of it watching television.

Your calendar should provide a good picture of your appointments, meetings, special events, vacations and times away from home. Every year this will change, especially if you have young children. Set a goal to try to carve out more free, unstructured time for yourself. My daughter Alexandra refers to this as "me time." Identifying how you spend your time, and all you're able to accomplish, gives you a healthy attitude about time. There is an abundance of hours, linked together. There *is* time when viewed properly. Our time alive is this precious gift of these golden hours. We have to be in control of just how carefully we parcel out this resource. But, no matter how thoughtfully we consider the great value of our time, there is very little if we are not exceedingly careful.

An hour never varies in duration, however or wherever you spend it. Write down the things you want to have time to do or do more of. Be as detailed as possible. Maybe you'd like to:

- ✽ Take a yoga class
- ✽ Go to the gym three times a week
- ✽ Read more
- ✽ Spend more time with your grandchildren
- ✽ Spend more time visiting with friends
- ✽ Go to museum exhibitions
- ✽ Spend more time with your children
- ✽ Do volunteer work
- ✽ Take up photography
- ✽ Spend more time communing with nature
- ✽ Meditate daily
- ✽ Have more free time
- ✽ Clear away clutter
- ✽ Study anthropology
- ✽ Learn to cook a new cuisine
- ✽ Visit different restaurants

We all need to claim our "me time." We need time to think, to contemplate, and to expand our perspective. These hours should not be spent in busyness with distractions and interruptions. When we're trying to focus our energies on one thing, it causes pressure and strain to be pulled in other directions. With careful planning, assume we have approximately five free hours a day—this adds up to thirty-five hours a week, one hundred forty hours a month, one thousand six hundred eighty golden, free hours a year. Hours accumulate. In five years, we'll have eight thousand, four hundred free hours. In these free hours, you can do a significant project—you can do some writing, create a garden, paint or study ancient Greek and Roman philosophy. You have these hours. Make time for what is important to you.

✽

TO FINISH THE MOMENT, TO FIND THE JOURNEY'S END IN EVERY STEP OF THE
ROAD, TO LIVE THE GREATEST NUMBER OF GOOD HOURS, IS WISDOM.

EMERSON

Avoiding the Pitfalls of Wasted Time

IT IS A MOST MORTIFYING REFLECTION FOR ANY MAN TO CONSIDER WHAT
HE HAS DONE COMPARED WITH WHAT HE MIGHT HAVE DONE.

SAMUEL JOHNSON

*I*n order to enjoy and celebrate as many good hours as humanly possible, we have to establish an inner-centered attitude about time. Even when we're fortunate to claim some time for ourselves, unless we can control the thoughts going through our minds, we are not free. Time is not ours unless we're able to think constructively and clearly about the importance of our short lifetime.

The more pure our mind, the more expansive and insightful our hours will become. Many of the time wasters that immediately come to mind are things we can avoid if we choose:

- Holding a grudge
- Gambling
- Worrying
- Being angry
- Gossiping
- Being petty
- Unhealthy habits
- Refusing to plan ahead
- Accepting the wrong job
- Marrying the wrong person
- Overdoing perfectionism
- Spoiling a child
- Living in messy rooms

✻ Proving you're right every time
✻ Bickering
✻ Holding on to a miserable situation
✻ Telling lies and covering them up

One of the biggest wastes of our time is to let other people manipulate us. There are many misguided people who feel they can demand things from us, who have no right to. They often pressure us to give a command performance. Some families feel they can demand their children make every effort possible to show up for Sunday dinner. A daughter drove five hours in freezing rain to go to a holiday dinner at her mother's house three states away. After dinner she drove home in a snowstorm in order to go to work on Monday morning. One Labor Day weekend when we'd rented a house in Nantucket, my mother tried to force me to leave our last weekend there to go to a family reunion. When I refused to ruin our vacation, she was furious. I had to stand firm in the face of her anger. Whenever we allow ourselves to be outer-directed about our time alive, we become victims of the tyranny of someone else's attempts to control us.

When we spend time with someone, we should give the encounter 100 percent of our focused energy. When we're prepared—in mind, body and spirit—we'll be co-creators in a pleasant, meaningful exchange, experiencing the heart of time.

We should try to live by the Golden Rule, being sensitive to just how invaluable other people's time is to them. Wasting someone else's time can be sinful. There is a huge difference between spending someone else's time productively and pleasurably, and wasting it. Having this sensitivity to others shows compassion. We want to be perceptive about the lives of others, trying never to impose. Whenever we ask more of someone else's time than they are freely willing to give us, we should back off. What we want from someone at a specific time might not be an appropriate request. Take their no gracefully. Our idea of productive or free time may not necessarily be the same as someone else's.

✻

DOST THOU LOVE LIFE? THEN DO NOT SQUANDER TIME,
FOR THAT'S THE STUFF LIFE IS MADE OF.

BENJAMIN FRANKLIN

Seize and Stretch Time

WAKE UP AND SEE FOR YOURSELF, WITH YOUR OWN EYES,
ALL YOU DREAMED OF, ALL YOUR DAYS!

HOMER

*T*here are big blocks of time and small snippets. All time is important. The best way to get the most out of every day is to make the best use of the "in-between" times. These interstices—small spaces of time between other activities—can be enormously productive when we grasp hold of sixty-second minutes.

Think what you can do in a minute: You can prepare a pot of coffee and turn on the machine. You can check your phone messages or email. You can send a fax. You can address an envelope and put a stamp on it. You can change a diaper. You can put a load of laundry into the washing machine.

The greater our spontaneity, the more we can seize and stretch these small, brief amounts of time. The key is to *do it now*. Paradoxically, we can accomplish a number of easy, routine tasks in no time when we're not excessively methodical, preplanning everything. We gain energy from variety. Vary the kind of short projects, as well as their locations. I can gladly spend a few minutes organizing my clothes closet, straightening out my shoes. I'll happily go to the laundry room in our apartment and iron a blouse. A few minutes later I might clean the bathroom floor while drawing a bath. Often I throw some stockings into the sink with a bar of scented soap so I can wash and rinse them while I'm waiting to have a bath. A friend actually cleans the shower while she is *in* the shower!

When I'm trying to accumulate longer periods of time, I use these little snatches of time to do what I have to do in the hopes that these tasks won't interfere with my larger, more expansive stretches of time. I'd rather pay a bill immediately in a two-minute slot than have to devote an hour or more to bill paying.

Another simple and practical way to stretch time is to always, with no exception, carry reading material. Bring with you to an appointment a newspaper article you've clipped to read when you have a free minute. Bring a magazine or paperback book with you. Whenever I have a doctor's appointment, I carry a file folder of work with me because I know from experience I'm often kept waiting.

There are so many ways we can vitalize our waiting time. When I arrive in the kitchen to prepare breakfast, I listen to inspirational tapes before Peter joins me. While standing waiting for a train or bus, we can do isometric exercises. When I'm meeting someone at a restaurant, I bring a few stamped, addressed museum postcards, so I can jot a note to a friend or child while I wait.

A great, easy and fast way to save time and never lose a good thought is to always carry a small notebook, 3 x 5 file card, or Post-it Notes. Relieve emotional stress and anxiety by always writing things down. Why tax your memory? When I'm in a taxi, I can make a list of things I want to do that day. I can plan what I'm going to pack for a trip a few days later. Whenever we write things down, we remember them better. I always take notes at lectures, seminars and religious services.

When Alexandra and Brooke were young, I made a habit of jotting down the adorable things they'd say wherever we were. I recorded these gems in tiny spiral notebooks I saved in a desk drawer. Our minds are swirling with thoughts all the time. Some people think a really good thought is never lost and will resurface if it is wise and wonderful, but I disagree. I write down impressions, ideas and insights, as well as what I need at the grocery store. Why have to go back for eggs—or search for a thought—and spend double the time?

I keep a punch list for each of my projects of all the little, often pesky, details that need attention. It frees my mind from being cluttered with these concerns when I'm concentrating on other projects. When I attend to the list, the process goes fast: boom, boom, boom! Our lives are full of countless details. Writing things down and keeping good files frees us to move easily from one thing to another without confusion or frustration.

By seizing and stretching the minutes, we're able to accomplish an enormous amount in the course of a day, feeling good about what we've accomplished, feeling on top of time. Whenever we make the most of everything we have, we feel satisfied and happy.

❋

VERY OFTEN THE POETIC VISION COMES SLOWLY, BIT BY BIT,
LIKE A SCENE SET ON THE STAGE. AT OTHER TIMES, HOWEVER,
IT IS SUDDEN AND FLEETING. SOMETHING PASSES BEFORE YOUR EYES,
AND IT MUST BE SEIZED QUICKLY OR IT IS LOST.

GUSTAVE FLAUBERT

Time Is Your Life

THE EVENTS IN OUR LIVES HAPPEN IN A SEQUENCE IN TIME,
BUT IN THEIR SIGNIFICANCE TO OURSELVES, THEY FIND THEIR OWN
ORDER ... THEIR CONTINUOUS THREAD OF REVELATION.

EUDORA WELTY

*T*ime is the substance of our lives. We are not of time but in time, as the late Eric Butterworth, a spiritual guide and teacher, taught us. We create our lives in time. The time is always now, the space is always here to live intensely. Only in our time alive will we be bound by time's reality.

There is time. That's all there is. Time is ours to embrace. None of us understands time fully, but we're vividly aware that it moves in one direction. This time continuum is nonspatial, and events occur in apparently irreversible succession from the past, through the present, to the future. As we become more conscious of how quickly our life advances, we must make time to take stock of our lives.

Are you taking advantage of all the time that is available to you? Have you found your passion and do you value your time as the most precious gem on earth? Our time alive should be a period of continuous activity and engagement.

A useful way to contemplate our time alive is as space to fill. An empty cup can be filled with tea. A piece of land can provide space to build a house. In time we have spaciousness to think, to produce, to act and to grow. How we fill our time mirrors our priorities and our destiny. Our goal should be to live well *every* day of our lives. Time gives us the space to experience the gift of opportunity. A professor, Robert Grudin, wrote an eloquent paragraph about life:

> *Happiness may well consist primarily of an attitude toward time. Individuals we consider happy commonly seem complete in the present: we see them constantly in their wholeness, attentive, cheerful, open rather than closed to events, integral in the moment rather than distended across time by regret or anxiety. Yet paradoxically they give an impression of permanence and consistency. They do not change greatly from day to day. They choose and patiently develop lengthy projects, so voluminous in time that the work of a single day is no more than a strand in the weft of a rug. They love remembering past experiences and making plans; they speak of past and future, not as external contexts, but rather as esteemed confederates, quiet extensions of their own being. One almost feels that their lives possess a kind of qualified eternity that past and future, birth and death, meet for them as in the completion of a circle.*

When we inhale, we are alive. Everything we do to improve ourselves and contribute to the world will be accomplished in time. Think tenderly on this. We're given this one lifetime as we know it. All else is a mystery. Let this period between two eternities be a significant time for you. What time is it? Now is the time. Set your clock now. Awaken to the rapture of being alive.

✻

YOU MUST UNDERSTAND THE WHOLE OF LIFE, NOT JUST ONE LITTLE PART OF IT. THAT IS WHY YOU MUST READ, THAT IS WHY YOU MUST LOOK AT THE SKIES, THAT IS WHY YOU MUST SING, AND DANCE, AND WRITE POEMS, AND SUFFER, AND UNDERSTAND, FOR ALL THAT IS LIFE.

J. KRISHNAMURTI

12

It Is Later Than You Think

TIME GOES, YOU SAY? AH NO! ALAS, TIME STAYS, WE GO.

HENRY AUSTIN DOBSON

*W*e're all in the boat of life together, sending our ship out to sail every day. We're all advancing toward the end of our earthly journeys. What we put into life comes back to us abundantly. Now is not the time to sit on the shore and wonder why life has passed us by.

Whether we're miserable or happy as a bird singing in the trees, you and I have only a few more precious years to live. We're not all blessed with radiant health to the end. Feel the power of your energy, what the Chinese call ch'i. Breathe in deeply. Slowly exhale. Don't be too concerned about how long you will live or what will happen after you die. Concentrate all your energies on how well you're living now, this moment, this day.

The current threats to our survival are reminders to us that there are no assurances of our being able to grow old. Live now, in this body, with your five senses. Enjoy the sensuality of human touch, reach out to a loved one with a hug, a kiss, a pat on the back. Savor your time with your partner and children. Let your loved ones know how much you adore them.

I've spent most of my life studying world religion and Eastern philosophy. I have a lot of questions and no complete answers about the nature of death, but I've learned a great deal about life. Ever since the age of three, when I became consciously aware I was alive, I've found my existence to be an exhilarating adventure. I love being here, now, in this body, where I'm able to eat, sleep, bathe, love, skip, dance, run, read, write and grow. Life becomes sweeter and more poignant with each fresh new dawn. I'm acutely aware how intensely passionate I am to be alive. I'm going to continue to live fully and with a flourish right to the end.

Heaven is not a location except in cartoons. Heaven is our happiness on earth, our love of life, our understanding of our life's sacredness. Here is where we create our paradise. In the eternal now, we can turn our lives into transcendent luminosity.

Treasure your life. Create triumphant celebrations. Lift the fog so you can experience the brilliant blue sky. Soak it all in and be grateful your two feet are on the ground! Yes, it is later than you think.

❀

THE CONFRONTATION WITH DEATH ... MAKES EVERYTHING LOOK SO PRECIOUS, SO SACRED, SO BEAUTIFUL THAT I FEEL MORE STRONGLY THAN EVER THE IMPULSE TO LIVE IT, TO EMBRACE IT, AND TO LET MYSELF BE OVERWHELMED BY IT.

ABRAHAM MASLOW

CHAPTER TWO

Home

13

Order Precedes Beauty

WE OURSELVES HAVE BOTH THE TASK AND THE PLEASURE OF ORGANIZING
AND SHAPING OUR LIVES FOR THE GOOD OF THE SOUL.

THOMAS MOORE

*W*ithout order there is no beauty. Living can be a messy business. The more engaged we are in living fully and well, the more stuff we seem to accumulate. We live in an orderly universe. Our homes and offices need to be kept orderly so we can spend our time in beautiful spaces that answer all our needs, arranged so that everything is both practical and uplifting.

To accomplish our goal to spend time in attractive, highly personal spaces that inspire our minds and engage our souls, we need to set up systems. When we have a place for everything and can free ourselves from disorder, we're more mentally alert, more receptive to new insights and our time is more fruitful. We can create a comprehensible arrangement for our possessions we need to store. A cook needs the spices close at hand. The way we use our space dictates the systematic placement of things to fill our functional needs. When we think through the logic, we produce freedom and harmony from discord.

Whether you are organizing clothes, toys, your kitchen, books or files, first walk through the space, creating scenarios of how you best function. How many different storage spaces do you have to access in order to set the table? Are the diapers for your baby a convenient hand's reach from the changing table? Are the towels near enough to the bathtub so you don't have to take your eye off a child when you reach for one?

Every aspect of your life can have more order to give you pleasure. Most of us are good about putting rarely used pots, pans, clothes and files in less accessible places to free up the nearby storage space for the things we use every day. But we have blind spots. We store napkins in one drawer and placemats in another. Silver is in a box, china is in a separate cabinet and glasses are in the kitchen cupboard. No wonder people seldom use their dining rooms!

Peter extends his desire for order to a useful bit of advice he calls "the ticket pocket theory" he learned from his uncle when he was fifteen. It has stood him in good stead ever since. In men's jackets there is a small inner pocket within the larger one. Uncle Jay told Peter to always put his tickets in this pocket. No fumbling, no mumbling, no slapping chest and trouser pockets. If the tickets are not in this pocket, they are not on his person.

An editor once asked me what she should do with all her pieces of paper with notes on them. I suggested that she get a loose-leaf notebook called a Filofax so that she could have one size of paper for every notation. I think I'd go mad if I had piles of random notes in stacks lying around, making me feel scattered.

Set up your own system in every area of your home and your life. Bring order out of clutter and clean things up. Albert Einstein gave us three rules of organizing our work: (1) Out of clutter, find simplicity; (2) From discord, find harmony; (3) In the middle of difficulty lies opportunity. Thomas Moore, author of *Care of the Soul*, believes that both the task and pleasure of organizing and shaping our lives nurtures the soul. The Japanese have a key expression: "Space to breathe." Through order, simplicity and harmony, we create this space to breathe. We can breathe more deeply when we remove thoughtless clutter.

I have a favorite expression: "de-thugging." When we attack our mess, we clean our mind as well as our spaces. Just as pruning and deadheading is soothing to do in a garden, we do the same with similar satisfaction in the drawers, closets, cabinets and cupboards in our spaces.

In our study there is a peek-in closet with shelves. I found a box for the closet with a pretty marbleized pattern that is exactly the right height and width to store my collection of meditation tapes. I smile as I see, feel, and sense that through order beauty is revealed.

We want to invest our time, to spend it wisely, to put it to excellent use. Clutter clogs our mind, dampens our spirit and takes a large portion of our limited time away from us.

❀

HOW MANY OF OUR DEMANDS COULD BE REDUCED IF WE PUT SOME ENERGY INTO PRIORITIZING, ORGANIZING, AND STREAMLINING THE ROUTINES THAT NOW FRITTER AWAY OUR ATTENTION?

MIHALY CSIKSZENTMIHALYI

14

Your Bedroom Is Your Sanctuary

ALL ONE REALLY NEEDS IS A DIVINELY ATTRACTIVE BED.

C. Z. GUEST

O ur home is our paradise on earth and our sacred place. Our bedroom is our private world of retreat, our intimate space, our sanctuary. When we enter our bedroom we should feel peaceful and protected. We spend one third of our life in this one room, more than in any other personal space, more than at an office. Our time in the bathroom becomes part of our bedroom time because the two rooms are closely connected. In these intimate spaces we retreat, we undress, we bathe, we touch, we contemplate, we heal, and we love. Our bedroom is the last impression we have before we shut our eyes to sleep, to dream. We awaken to a new day in this same atmosphere. This environment has a great deal of influence on our mind, our heart, our body and our soul.

Bedrooms should be tender and sweet. We should invest our time in this personal space away from random outside influences. Here, in quiet, we confront our true selves. We select who we speak with on the telephone, we select what music we listen to, we choose a place to meditate or do yoga stretches or to read inspirational books. Having a live tree, flowering plant, or fresh-cut flowers in our bedroom keeps us in touch with nature.

I've helped decorate many bedrooms in my interior design career and the ones I feel are the most beautiful are really quite simple. One comes immediately to mind: a friend's bedroom in Texas. The walls and ceiling are cornflower blue with shiny white trim, the canvas curtains are hand-painted with irregular stripes in many soft shades of blue with white. The posts of the four-poster bed were designed to look like tree trunks in a soft yellow oak tone. The bed linens and pillows are crisp white with blue scalloped edges. The bed dominates the room. There is no television, no visible technology. There are some favorite paintings and a wonderful blue and white quilt folded at the foot of the bed.

Keep your bedroom crisp and uncluttered. Try to have any necessary storage in an attractive chest of drawers or in armoires. When you enter this space, you are going to spend soulful time alive.

❀

'EVERYTHING IN A BEDROOM SHOULD CONTRIBUTE
TO AN ATMOSPHERE OF PEACE.

BILLY BALDWIN

15

You Create Your Spirit of Place

EACH PLACE HAS A SPIRIT OF ITS OWN WHICH
PROGRESSIVELY SHAPES ITS PHYSICAL APPEARANCE AND THE GENIUS
OF ITS PEOPLE.

RENÉ DUBOS

I like to show people how they can design happiness into their lives through their homes. While it is true that each specific place has a distinctive genius, just as with each individual person, an ideal spirit of place has to be created. I think of Paris, Provence, Venice, Tuscany, Florence, Rome, Maine, Colorado, La Jolla and Stonington Village as ideal places. What places come to your mind?

We're continuously infusing our vital energy and our creative juices into where and how we live, shaping the invisible forces that make a place unique. The spirit of place that engages our soul has an atmosphere that is gentle, pure and subtle, with hidden dimensions of meaning, integrity, authenticity and exceptional charm. The places where we love to go can be our inspiration to bring some of the same light, color and textures into our own homes, lending an echo of other places that have captured our hearts.

Develop a philosophy of place as you go about your life. Alert yourself to pick out places that have the most positive energy—that have strength, and give you a sense of vigor. What are some ideal settings for you? Where do you most love to be? How do these spaces change at different times of day or types of weather? What are some of the wonderful places where you feel most inspired? Visualize the atmosphere. When you experience places you particularly love, think about how these environments make you feel. Describe the elements in order to try to emulate them in your own homes or apartments.

Places with the most positive energy leave us with a feeling of enchantment. Each of us brings our own values, experiences and exposure to our homes. I'm most comfortable and happy in an atmosphere that is light, airy and bright, that is also relaxed, cheerful, charming, simple and earthy. Rigid formality and strict structure make me feel awkward and anxious.

I often write about my favorite living artist, Roger Mühl, who paints scenes that have great spirit of place. Whether he paints a simple house near the water, rooftops, trees, sun-drenched gardens, or winding secret paths, through color he awakens us to the vibrant beauty of nature as well as to the joy of everyday life at home and in our surroundings. The Mediterranean sky he paints is sometimes so intense that objects seem to be lit from within. Whether the scene is indoors or out in plain air, he encourages us to see and feel and live exuberantly. A flower vase brims with pink tulips or red roses. Fruit ripens in a bowl. He paints what delights his senses right in front of his eyes.

One of my favorite Mühl paintings is of a table on his terrace overlooking his garden in Provence. The setting is late afternoon after a feast of bouillabaisse, cooked outside from the freshest gifts from the Mediterranean a few kilometers away. There are glasses half full of red and white wine, French bread, a platter of cheese, jugs of wine, apricot and apple fruit tarts. We, the spectators, yearn to be there. We want to savor the banquet, enjoy the friendship, feel uplifted by the conversation, linger over the laughter. This sense of immediacy, of life being celebrated now, has an intoxicating vitality.

When we love the beauty of nature—the sun, sky, water, grass, trees, flowers, fruits and vegetables—we can bring this energy, color and liveliness inside, where we live. We don't all experience an artistic life in Provence, but my friends in Atlanta have named their screened-in porch their "Provence room." There they envision sensuous delight and leave their cares behind.

According to the Chinese doctrine known as feng shui—wind and water—the buildings where we live and work should be exposed to attractive views and be located near farmlands, streams and trees. We know emotionally what feeds our soul and makes us content. We should always strive to have a spirit of place where there is an intimate connection between us and our environment.

Our homes can and should be places with great spirit, an atmosphere that encourages us to make our daily lives a work of art, bringing us continual joy. We constantly influence our homes as we create a spirit of place. As we evolve, as we improve our physical spaces, we in turn are being shaped by our environment. This creative process of connecting ourselves and our family to our private spaces continues throughout our lives. We are not only influenced by the natural forces of our environment, but also by social and psychological surroundings that we choose and create. We first select our spirit of place, and over time, we gradually become who we are because of the quality of the experiences we have in this chosen environment.

When we set out to create a spirit of place, this process involves many factors other than the landscape, seascape, geographical location and architecture. We develop patterns of behavior, express our tastes and exercise our free will to express our individuality—something we prize above all else. No two human beings are alike. We want to live the way we please. Our living spaces should both reflect and enhance what pleases us most.

Even when you're not there, the place you created with your spirit is there for you. Your energy is there. The time you actually spend in a space may be a small percentage of your time, but the emotional impact of being there is enormous. We inherit the spirit of a place. The genius of place shapes us.

❀

THERE IS NO VALUE IN LIFE EXCEPT WHAT YOU CHOOSE
TO PLACE UPON IT AND NO HAPPINESS IN ANY PLACE EXCEPT
WHAT YOU BRING TO IT YOURSELF.

HENRY DAVID THOREAU

※ 16 ※

The Planet Is Your Home

LOVE ALL OF CREATION, THE WHOLE AND EVERY GRAIN OF SAND IN IT.
LOVE EVERY LEAF, EVERY RAY OF LIGHT. LOVE THE ANIMALS, LOVE THE
PLANTS, LOVE EVERY THING. IF YOU LOVE EVERYTHING, YOU WILL PERCEIVE
THE DIVINE MYSTERY IN THINGS. ONCE YOU PERCEIVE IT, YOU WILL BEGIN
TO COMPREHEND IT BETTER EVERY DAY. AND YOU WILL COME AT LAST
TO LOVE THE WHOLE WORLD WITH AN ALL-EMBRACING LOVE.

DOSTOYEVSKY

*M*y trip around the world with my aunt when I was sixteen continues to influence the entire direction of my life. Travel sharpens our worldview, makes us understand our connectedness and deepens our understanding of ourselves. While it is true that we learn about other customs and cultures from visiting other countries, I've never left home without gaining a deeper sense of who I am.

A reader wrote me a curious letter years ago: she asked if I love home so passionately, why do I travel so much? Our planet is teeming with life and energy, adventure, gifts of wonder, color, interesting people, places and things. The sheer exhilaration of immersing ourselves in another place, blending in and learning about another culture, eating new foods, and absorbing the way of life, is a magical thrill. Every place on earth is authentic, with its own unique cultural character.

In addition to taking me around the world at such an impressionable age, my aunt left me a thousand dollars in her will. She died of a heart attack when she was sixty years old and I was thirty. I had two young daughters and worked for an interior design firm in New York. Guess what I did with the thousand dollars? I started a travel fund. I made a commitment to myself to follow her example and to make the planet my home. My passport is always near at hand.

The head of the design firm where I worked encouraged me and the other young designers to go to Europe at least once a year to expose our eyes and minds to noble architecture and ideal scale, proportion and beautiful scenery, and to inspire our work by experiencing different ways of life. Because of these two women, Aunt Betty and Mrs. Brown, I ended up decorating internationally because I wasn't afraid of differences; rather, I embraced them.

When the ambassador to the United States from Singapore invited me to do the interior design work for his country's permanent residence in New York City, I offered to go to Singapore and do research because I'd never been there before. Ambassador Koh sent me on a three-month trip throughout Southeast Asia—a thrill that will never fade because when he asked me to bring one assistant, I brought my husband, Peter. Visiting different countries as a tourist is one thing, but traveling with a sense of purpose and focus, as well as being hosted by the ambassador and his wife and friends, made our experience so much more educational and meaningful.

The English writer Lawrence Durrell's collection of travel essays, *Spirit of Place*, reminds me that all places derive their uniqueness from hidden forces. We remember the mood of a place because of its spirit. This nonmaterial force is beyond our five senses. We always respond emotionally to the distinctive characteristics of a place.

The planet is vast and there is too much to see to spend time in ho-hum, humdrum places. You shouldn't be limited to where you were born and raised.

Few of us can find such ecstasy in living as the reclusive poet Emily Dickinson that we can do without exploring the world and participating in this great adventure. We can fly everywhere and enjoy the whole planet. We are a part of the globe. Broaden your horizons and plan an exciting trip to an exotic, far-off place.

What are your five favorite countries? What are your favorite cities? What are some of your favorite islands? What are some of your favorite mountains? Do you prefer to visit cities with museums and restaurants and shops to being in rural areas? Does it depend specifically what country you're thinking about? Take the time to visit a variety of places—it will enrich your life. Doesn't a year always seem to last longer when you have taken some trips?

❀

A WISE MAN FEELS AT HOME IN EVERY COUNTRY.
THE WHOLE UNIVERSE IS THE HOME OF A NOBLE SOUL.

DEMOCRITUS

17

Trust Your Eye

GAZING ON BEAUTIFUL THINGS ACTS ON MY SOUL.

MICHELANGELO

Our time alive can be greatly enriched by the quality of our ability to see beauty. To see well is to live well. The more beauty we expose ourselves to, the more we are absorbing the most we can from every moment.

My eyes may be my greatest gift. As a young gardener I looked keenly at the seedlings, the sprouts and blossoms, with a sense of magical wonder at creation. When I chose to become an interior designer, my role was not just to be able to see and appreciate what is beautiful, but I had to be able to envision how a space would look, as well as imagine how the design transformation would feel to my client. Being able to look and really see well is a gift, but whatever our natural inheritance, we can train our eye and should concentrate on seeing with deeper sensitivity throughout our lives.

One evening when I was hanging a collection of botanical watercolors for clients, they were shocked to discover that I didn't measure anything. I'd had all the frames made alike and because each flower was a different scale and proportion as well as color, my eye had to decide where to place them. Recently we were hanging large watercolor paintings together and we had many laughs because I noticed that both clients now trusted their eyes. I felt my role now was to admire where they felt the paintings should be hung.

To boost your confidence, consider taking photographs of what is most beautiful to you. You will intuitively photograph what you are attracted to. The great thing about a photo is its ability to arrest the moment, to capture an experience that will never come again. I don't need to encourage parents to take photos of their children and friends. We do this instinctively, but we can gain tremendous confidence in our ability to see well when we photograph beauty and poignancy in all the everyday scenes around us:

❋ A blue hydrangea bush hugging a picket fence
❋ A sunrise
❋ Light on the water
❋ Birds in flight
❋ Sunlight dappling through trees
❋ A table setting
❋ Fresh flowers in a vase in natural light
❋ Lilac trees in bloom against a blue sky
❋ Crocus sprouting through snow in the sunlight
❋ Fresh fruit, vegetables and flowers at the farmers' market
❋ A townhouse with geraniums in window boxes

When the French artist and photojournalist Henri Cartier-Bresson died in 2004 at the age of ninety-five, we learned about his genius in his own words, as well as in the photographs and drawings he left behind. His clarity of vision, his ability to see the geometry of a fleeting image, was brilliant. He encourages us to think of ourselves as artists: "Anyone with sensitivity is potentially an artist. But then you must have concentration." In 1931 while recuperating in Marseilles from blackwater fever, he bought his first Leica camera, the kind he used for the rest of his life. "I prowled the streets all day, feeling strung up and ready to pounce, determined to 'trap life'—to preserve life in the act of living."

Taking photographs awakens our soul. He suggests we "approach tenderly, gently . . . on tiptoe—even if the subject is a still life, a velvet hand, a hawk's eye—these we should all have." From the pictures you choose to take, you'll see that you believe the world to be miraculous. As William Wordsworth reminds us, "My heart leaps up when I behold a rainbow in the sky."

Our perception is a wellspring of clarity in helping us to perceive, to understand and to love life. Cartier-Bresson teaches us, "In whatever one does, there must be a relationship between the eye and the heart. One must come to one's subject in a pure spirit. One must be strict with oneself. There must be time for contemplation, for reflection about the world and the people about one. If one photographs people, it is their inner look that must be revealed."

Whether we carry a small portable camera with us or we merely use our eyes to awaken to all the beauty around us, when we trust our eyes, we trust what is beautiful in our hearts. When we truly see, we know the truth. Our eye, like a camera, doesn't lie.

✳

NOTHING HERE BELOW IS PROFANE FOR THOSE WHO KNOW
HOW TO SEE. ON THE CONTRARY, EVERYTHING IS SACRED.

PIERRE TEILHARD DE CHARDIN

18

Lower Your Standards

TRANQUILITY IS MORE IMPORTANT THAN PERFECTION.

GRETA K. NAGEL

*I*f you are trying to carve out more free time for yourself, reevaluate your maintenance standards. We all know how satisfying it feels to have everything in working order and our household running smoothly, but when people have insanely high standards, little time is left for self-development, or time to goof off.

Our home is our intimate sacred place. There is a time to spruce up and there is a time to flop down on a sofa with our feet up and enjoy our coffee and a good book. Home shouldn't be a work trap or a burden; we are privileged to have a roof over our head, even when it leaks in a heavy rainstorm.

Many people pride themselves on being perfectionists, but when standards are taken too far, they become an excessive burden. Anything—positive or negative—can be carried to extreme. We should strive to do our best but not abuse ourselves with the pressures of expecting everything to be perfect. The *American Heritage Dictionary* describes perfectionism as "having a propensity for being displeased with anything that is not perfect or does not meet extremely high standards." I've chosen to lower my standards, and I recommend this decision to anyone who wants to celebrate life fully every moment.

I love our apartment and cottage so much that I try never to feel the burdens of maintenance. Ever since the sixties when I started writing, I always choose to train my mind before I do housework. As much as I enjoy having our home clean and well ordered, I put my own growth as a priority. Once I've studied and learned something profound, I'm energetic and can use my positive energy to tidy up and clean my environment. If I did all that could or should be done before I began my work, I would never accomplish my goals.

We all want to feel that we have a sense of control, but we can become obsessed by trying to have our home immaculate at all times. Leaves will continue to fall from the trees, so the lawn isn't perfect. The kitchen sink always has something in it, and the laundry and ironing are never done. Houses are meant to be lived in! Living is a messy business. We have to learn to relax when the bed isn't made and the living room rug needs to be vacuumed. A house that is always party-ready might not be a loving, family-centered home. We must take time off from maintaining to live.

Keep in mind Parkinson's Law: work expands so as to fill the time available for its completion. Be careful to walk away from housework regularly. Do your creative, fun work and play first. Have specific times when you do whatever you wish to do, regardless of what you could do. You are the master of your time. What can you do today that will outlive you? Begin it. What can you do right now that you'd love to do? What is keeping you from acting on your desires?

You are not a housekeeper. You do housework because it is necessary to be done, but it should not interfere with your personal interests and need to express yourself. Just because you can doesn't mean you should.

The paradox is that in order to celebrate life every day, we have to train ourselves to be able to overlook things. While the house is being painted, we can look over the scaffolding, out to the water and boats in the harbor. Keep your energy positive. It's better to have half the loaf than none. When we are pleased with the very circumstances of our life just as they are—confusion and all—we enhance our pleasure in life.

❋

A WISE MAN SEES AS MUCH AS HE OUGHT, NOT AS MUCH AS HE CAN.

MONTAIGNE

19

Light the Lights

LIGHT IS IMMATERIAL. YOU GRAB IT WITH YOUR MIND, YOUR SOUL,
YOUR HEART. I THINK OF IT AS A FRIENDLY GHOST THAT SURROUNDS US.

INGO MAWER

I worship light; light is our life, our existence. Let the light shine everywhere. When luminous light shines from the sun, partly concealed by white puffy clouds, we're able to see rays of divine light. Spiritually, the more light we have in our soul, the higher our consciousness. Praise all sources of light—the sun, a star, a candle, a fire, a lighthouse, an electric light bulb.

Some houses and apartments have abundant light because of climate and location. But many of us are light deprived, especially those of us who spend time indoors or who live in cities. Light is admitted through windows or windowpanes, skylights and glass doors. Most city apartments have limited windows that bring in direct sunlight.

On a magnificently dazzling sunny day in August, I was amazed how dark our apartment looked and felt. We have east-west exposures, but the brilliant sunshine streaming in the kitchen window in the early morning soon moved, so there was a sense of loss of vital energy.

I love to enjoy the light in the three east exposures—the kitchen, laundry room and our office, but I can't be in three rooms at once doing different tasks. What is the solution? By the time I'm finished in the kitchen, I've lost the light in the office, all before nine o'clock in the morning. The living room and our bedroom have two west windows, so the natural light comes in around seven in the evening during the summer months.

On that beautiful, bright August day, I was in artificially lit rooms for ten hours. Thanks to all the advances in lighting, I was able to see to do paperwork at my office desk and at my writing table in the living room. I went out for several hours to have lunch, to do some errands and to walk around to absorb the sunshine. The sun was ebullient. Colors were clear, the sky was deep bright blue. Exhilarated by being in the sunlight, I walked into the apartment and upon entering our hallway, I suddenly faced gloomy darkness because of lack of natural light. I immediately flicked on bright halogen overhead lights and full-spectrum pure white light bulbs. I poured myself some iced tea and sat at my writing table, eager to get to work. Full-spectrum bulbs give off all of the visible colors in sunlight, producing more contrast and sharper views. I looked around our pretty living room with its cheerful colors, flowers, paintings, and objects we love, and felt I was in a sunroom. My eyes were happy to be able to see clearly.

Light the lights. Most rooms are dimly lit, useless for hours of concentration where it should be pleasant to read and write. Remember, we are 90 percent light deprived when we are inside our rooms with normal illumination compared to being out of doors sitting under an umbrella on a sunny summer day. But because I don't do my paperwork outside in New York City, I must make sure our apartment is well lit.

I first began doing research on light and lighting in the 1970s. When light bulbs give off dim yellow light or we use fluorescent lighting that concentrates on the yellow-green portion of the spectrum, we don't feel as peppy as we do when the artificial light is full-spectrum, emulating the sun. We can't count on the sun to always shine through. We have foggy, cloudy rainy days. Winter months deprive us of light hours. In the time we have alive, we should concentrate our energies on seeing that we have ample light in our spaces. When we do, we're free to read in and enjoy all of our rooms.

In addition to full-spectrum light, we can place mirrors to reflect light, making rooms brighter. Mirrors are most useful opposite or next to windows, creating the illusion of more light and space.

Turn on extra lights on a stormy gray day. We can all make our own sun-rooms in our homes. When our rooms are sunny, we benefit from our time in these cheerful spaces. Good lighting enlightens our soul as it enlivens our home.

Light the lights and celebrate all your precious days. Let your light shine. When you lighten up, you brighten up.

❀

THERE ARE TWO WAYS OF SPREADING LIGHT: TO BE THE CANDLE OR
THE MIRROR THAT REFLECTS IT.

EDITH WHARTON

20

Freshen Up Your Rooms!

YOU ARE NOT SIMPLY CHANGING YOUR ENVIRONMENT, YOU ARE
TRANSFORMING YOUR LIFE.

WILLIAM SPEAR

*A*ll the bright lights in the world are no substitute for fresh, crisp, new fabrics. After five or ten years, our rooms begin to look tired. Because I'm a great advocate of having as much natural light as possible in the rooms we live in, our fabrics fade and their life force diminishes over time. We tend to spend less time in rooms that feel stale and dreary. This compounds the situation because any room we don't spend happy hours enjoying becomes a space with bad energy. We should laugh in our spaces, smile, talk lovingly to our objects, and sing to our plants. There are no inanimate objects that don't have hidden dimensions of spirit. The best room in your house is the room where you long to be.

Before you begin freshening up your rooms, pause, breathe deeply, and look around. I suggest you concentrate on one room at a time. A young mother from Chicago freshened up her three-year-old daughter's room and suddenly she felt her own bedroom lacked vitality. It seemed dull and color-less: white walls and off-white curtains. (I jokingly say that "off-white is 'off.'") When you view your rooms through this awareness, you'll see that perhaps the colorful flowered sheets are faded and not as crisp and clear as they once were, and the white bedspread is no longer bright. This is what Barbara noticed.

Her freshening-up project was relatively simple and inexpensive. She was able to buy crisp white curtains on sale at Target. She and her husband painted the walls bright white and the ceiling a pale cornflower blue. She treated herself to a new set of floral blue hydrangea sheets on a fresh white background. Using a simple white lightweight coverlet, she eliminated the tired old heavier one. She found some new lampshades and bought blue and white cotton rugs at Ikea for both sides of the bed. She added a wicker plant stand and put in some trailing English ivy. Now Barbara loves to sit on her bed and read when her daughter takes her afternoon nap.

The rule when freshening up a room is that one thing leads to another. You have to think of the room as a whole. If we think a few bright throw pillows will spiff up a faded sofa, we are kidding ourselves. They'll only showcase the sofa's sadness, and we'll lose the clarity and joy of a fresh, clean space.

Variety makes everything fresh and new. When we decide to freshen up our rooms, we usually think in terms of the fabrics and rugs, the textures and color of the textiles, not our wood pieces. But sometimes we look at a room and visualize different colored wood, or envision wanting to paint the furniture a color, or feel the floor stain is too dark or too light.

In a spiral notebook, make a master freshen-up plan, room by room. By focusing your time, energy and money on one room at a time, you can be sensitive about paying attention to all the possibilities and nuances with a sense of pleasure rather than feeling overwhelmed.

If now is not an appropriate time to freshen up one of your rooms, jot down ideas in your notebook of what you'd love to do when you are able. Clip out pictures of fabrics you've seen in magazines. Go to some stores and look around to see what's available, and what colors, textures and shapes excite you. Go to a plant store and buy a flowering plant or a tree for a room that needs help. Any move forward will keep you enthusiastic. When you are able to freshen up your rooms by adding something living and growing, your rooms instantly feel more refreshing. Having to water the plant or tree gives you the opportunity to appreciate the space and may inspire you to use it more.

I've never spent time in a room I couldn't improve. We get to know what's working and what's not from spending time living in a space. In time, the room will speak to you, and you will know what to do to enhance your life.

✳

CHANGE MAKES YOU SEE ANEW.

VALERIE STEELE

Put Your Rooms to Use

*T*he rooms we occupy are not still lifes. They are living, breathing spaces where we go to celebrate every day. While there will be many different rooms in our lives, each one we feel comfortable in and enjoy living in will have a great deal of influence on our mood and outlook.

Our rooms are our friends, our companions, our muse. They are there, patiently waiting to be occupied. How often do we stand at the entrance to a pretty room that we've enjoyed decorating and living in, and become aware of how much genuine happiness this space has provided for us and our loved ones?

The wise ancient Chinese sage Lao Tzu had an expression: "empty and be full." I've learned to leave an empty shelf in my linen closet so that I have a place for sheets and towels after they're folded in the laundry room. I have empty shelves in the library for future books. I try to keep empty drawers for new undergarments. Empty spaces are openings for a more graceful life.

A Zen master was sharing the tea ceremony with a pupil. The teacher deliberately poured tea into his student's cup until it spilled over and made a mess. When asked why he did this, the answer was clear: "When your mind is so full of preconceived notions, you have no room for insights and new inspiration."

Just as we have to be empty in order to become full, our rooms can't be so cramped with clutter and old newspapers and messy piles that we don't feel comfortable or inspired to put them to creative use. For most of us, the largest portion of our time is spent in our personally arranged rooms. They should fit our needs as attractively as a well-tailored suit fits our body.

I put my rooms to use and they all get a lot of wear and tear. I can't imagine one less room in my life. If I'm not in my Zen writing room, but looking at it from the adjoining upstairs library, it is there for me, ready with good energy, neat and receptive. The space is breathing. Even when I'm on an airplane en route to the West Coast, I'm able to envision my writing table, feel the smooth polished walnut in my imagination, and look forward to being there again.

The legendary interior decorator Elsie de Wolfe believed "in plenty of optimism and white paint, comfortable chairs with lights beside them, open fires on the hearth and flowers . . . mirrors and sunshine in all rooms." My friend, the icon of interior decoration, Billy Baldwin, believed, "As we approach a room it should lure us to enter and sit in it."

We should find living in all our spaces a delight. In my newly freshened-up laundry room, I have clear Lucite bins to hold clothes to be ironed and shirts to go to the dry cleaners. The Container Store sells bright white cardboard boxes the perfect size to hold cassette tapes. I enjoy listening to philosophy when I'm ironing, doing laundry, or sewing on a button. Because I have my Walkman, earphones, and tapes right there, I can purposefully double my benefit from these often short chunks of time by studying. I keep 3 x 5 cards, pencils, pens, and ink cartridges in a small white chest of drawers that I purchased at Hold Everything, so I can jot down notes if I'm inspired!

Every room should have a pad of paper and pencils or pens, and not just near a telephone. In a cup in the bathroom, keep some pens and pencils and a pad handy in case you get your best ideas while taking a nice long bath.

I collect decorative storage boxes in all sizes, shapes, colors and patterns. I love boxes because they're useful. I enjoy using pretty containers for storage, because having surfaces covered with belongings distracts me and makes me feel anxious. The key is to label the boxes so you can pick up a box and bring it with you to whatever room you decide to work in, depending on your mood, the project, the time of day, your sense of privacy, and how much space you'll need to feel comfortable.

While I am guilty of having stacks of work in piles on my desks both in New York and at the cottage, I always begin writing on a clear, clean surface. I try to empty my mind in order to be full.

Try to have space on your tabletops, especially the coffee table. We increased the usefulness of our kitchen substantially when we purchased a large table from Crate & Barrel that we use for eating and working. When we dine, we light candles and turn on soft under-counter lights. When we work, we turn on a utilitarian full-spectrum gooseneck lamp with the light equivalent of a 250-watt bulb (the energy used is similar to a 60-watt bulb). To increase the usefulness of your rooms, keep in mind:

- ❈ Empty and be full
- ❈ Have space to breathe
- ❈ Have clear, clean surfaces
- ❈ Use attractive boxes for storage
- ❈ Have lots of white paint to add to the sense of openness and space
- ❈ Have books and current magazines handy
- ❈ Keep two good upholstered chairs with adequate reading light for each one
- ❈ Have sufficient space on a table next to a chair to put down a beverage, eyeglasses, and books
- ❈ When appropriate, have a large ottoman to put your feet up on, to perch on, to put a tray of drinks on, or for books and magazines
- ❈ Monitor television watching
- ❈ Have clean windows that open and close easily
- ❈ Have a view or favorite painting to look at, or preferably, both
- ❈ Bring fresh flowers or plants into your rooms
- ❈ Have a radio or CD player with a remote control

- ❋ Have framed photographs of children, treasured friends, and one of you when you were young and darling
- ❋ Have at least one of your treasured objects in each room
- ❋ Rearrange furniture seasonally
- ❋ Have a desk or writing table in the rooms where you love spending timeless moments

❋

WE CANNOT BE FILLED UNLESS WE ARE FIRST EMPTIED,
TO MAKE ROOM FOR WHAT IS TO COME.

THOMAS MERTON

The Surprise of a Home Vacation

THE PATH IS BEAUTIFUL AND PLEASANT
AND JOYFUL AND FAMILIAR.

MEISTER ECKHART

$\mathcal{A}$ s much as I love to travel and explore the world, life is never sweeter than when we return home, where we feel comforted by our familiar things, where we're able to sleep in our own bed. Whenever I go on a business trip or vacation I open the front door upon returning home and feel the blessings of living in spaces I love. I gain a renewed love of home that is stimulated by spending time away. In my case, absence *does* make my heart grow fonder. I tend to see everything I love as though for the first time.

Since acquiring our sweet eighteenth-century cottage, Peter and I have chosen to take home vacations. We always do this in the summer, and we try to squeeze in one in the heart of winter. We have a glorious time, doing whatever we feel like doing, as the spirit moves us. This is not a family vacation; this is a special time for us to sensuously enjoy our home and tenderly be together.

What would you do on a home vacation? Have breakfast in bed? Read the entire newspaper? Not read the newspaper? Finish a craft project? Take afternoon siestas? Have picnics on your porch or at the beach? Sip your afternoon tea by the fire or in the garden? Go on five-mile walks every evening before dinner? Read a classic you've been putting off for a year? Paint a room with your spouse? Plant flower bulbs? Polish the brass?

Let your imagination run wild. The timing and duration are entirely up to you—perhaps a long weekend or up to a week when your children go off to school or camp, or to visit with their grandparents. You will have to make some changes in order to assure the most enjoyable home vacation imaginable. Beforehand, make lunch and dinner reservations at restaurants in your region. Depending on where you live and the climate, you might want to take a picnic to a beach, but the whole idea is to have a faux escape at home. You're fully there, but with a refreshed appreciation.

You may have your breakfast at home, but arranged as you would be likely to find it at an inn, a bed and breakfast, or a hotel. Ahead of time, stock up on fresh flowers, fruit, good coffee, magazines and books you've intended to read for months.

Pretend you're in the most luxurious inn in the world. Call your bedroom Room Number One. Have your prettiest sheets on the bed, a pitcher of colorful flowers, magazines and books, a scented candle and favorite nightwear and robes. You are now in your private world of retreat. Screen your telephone calls, turn off the cell phone and television, and drift away to a dreamland.

You have absolute privacy—no tap, tap on your bedroom door. You have all your favorite things around you. You don't have to acclimate to new places and people. You suffer no disorientation from jet lag or surprising (often inordinate) expenses. You experience no travel time, no security check, no lost passport, no hassle, no suitcases to pack, unpack and pack again. You have enough hangers. You know where the bathroom is in the middle of the night.

There is no tipping at home. You have your favorite, inspiring music. You know the good views, the best walking paths, the times of day when the terrace is the most pleasant. The roses are from your own garden. You feel the powerful connection between you and your beloved home.

Temporarily you leave the Windex under the kitchen sink. No matter how much you love to cook, no one enjoys preparing, cooking and cleaning up eighty-four meals a month. This is your time to be seated and served, letting others cook for you and wait on you hand and foot. Depending on where you live, you can have a massage or have your hair styled or cut. You can play tennis, go to a play in a park, go to an art show or local museum. The whole idea is to spend sacred time at home.

When you take a home vacation, you freshly recognize that your daily life is sublime. You discover that you actually enjoy the little domestic chores you now see as grace notes. You widen your perspective and feel the awakening of your soul to how beautiful and meaningful your home is and how precious your time alive is. And best of all: no hotel bill!

❋

THERE'S NO PLACE LIKE HOME.

DOROTHY IN *THE WIZARD OF OZ*

Be Happy at Home

COMING HOME IS A VISUAL BANQUET: A METAPHOR OF JOURNEY, DESTINY
AND LOVE. HERE IS WHERE WE ARE OURSELVES—WHERE WE LONG TO BE.

PETER MEGARGEE BROWN

*Y*our lifetime is primarily enjoyed in your home. Where else can you be happier than in the privacy of the environment you love? Your own home! What a blessing to know we can live joyfully in our own home, letting the mystery, magic, wonder and power of the spirit of place feed our soul.

Shouldn't we all love our homes? My adorable twin grandchildren love to say "my car," "my book," "my room," "my shoes," "my house," "my dog," "my bike." I've never been in anyone else's house that could possibly make me as content and fully alive as being in our own home. No matter how pretty and comfortable someone else's life is, I'm always aware I am a guest, a temporary visitor in someone else's home. The colors, textures, favorite things, are interesting and charming, but they don't hold personal meaning to me, they don't tell my story or sing my song. Eventually we want to return home to our own daily life, to our own familiar things, to our own customs and preferred style of life.

I'm an absolute believer that no matter how satisfied we are, no matter how much we love our home, we can always improve the quality of our time spent in this most sacred of places. There are always so many imaginative ways we can increase our love of home. We'll never arrive at a time and place when we feel we have finished the decoration and organization of our house.

Everything in life is a process of discovery. Everything is constantly changing, evolving and transcending. So it is with our home, as it reflects us. Nothing will be just right forever. We continuously make little adjustments, find new favorite places to enjoy, where we're free to do productive things we love:

✲   Read in the living room swivel chair facing the harbor
    to be able to glance up from a book and watch the sunset
✲   Arrange flowers in the laundry room
✲   Eat in the living room by the fire
✲   Wrap holiday presents in the dining room by the fire
✲   Sit under the umbrella in the backyard on sunny days
    and read and write
✲   Plan a nap for yourself in the afternoon
✲   Establish family reading times
✲   Have the children cook one dinner a week
✲   Claim quiet times throughout the day

Being happy at home is an accomplishment. Sadly, too few people find domestic bliss. The home is not often enough a place where there is peace and an atmosphere where we're encouraged to grow deeper spiritually and exercise our intellectual powers.

For many young parents with growing children, there is little, if any, time for reflection, relaxation and leisure. These are the most precious years of your life. Be sure you are enjoying them. In order to be happy at home you will need to claim regular breaks from the endless schedules and routine.

At this stage, my happiness at home is more quiet. I have raised my family. They have their own exciting lives to live. I now have more free time to contemplate, to read, to study and question deep philosophical, universal issues. Am I happier now than I was when my daughters were young, at home, and full of vitality, with the telephone always ringing, music blasting from each room, friends coming over, having meals together, laughter and tears shared? No. My happiness is different now. I am more contemplative because I have more free time, but all the memories of those exhilarating years as an active family live in my heart every moment.

No matter where we call home, no matter how young or old we are, we carry our happiness within our souls. Nothing looks or feels beautiful when we are unhappy. When we love who we are inside, when we love the life we have chosen to live, when we're inner-directed in our thoughts and actions, we can handle the rough patches and the really difficult times. We *can* be happy at home through all of life's passages.

❋

THE HAPPIEST MOMENTS OF MY LIFE HAVE BEEN THE FEW WHICH
I HAVE PASSED AT HOME IN THE BOSOM OF MY FAMILY.

THOMAS JEFFERSON

Your Home Environment
Is Your Life Story

THE MORE I EXPLORED, THE MORE ABSORBED I BECAME
WITH THE MYSTERY OF ENVIRONMENT.

ALEXANDER LIBERMAN

*L*ook around your home. Every object has a story. Our home evolves and changes every day we spend time living and enjoying ourselves in our rooms. Everything has importance. When we walk through our spaces, we see ourselves in the things we've selected to live with, in the art we collect, in the treasured objects that we've inherited or that have been given to us by loved ones.

It takes a lifetime to bring together all the furniture, paintings, books, china, crystal, linens, photographs and memorabilia. Everything is so personal, nostalgic and sentimental. As an interior designer, I've always tried to help my clients create personally meaningful environments where they feel a connection to all their objects. Everything should come from the heart, because when an object speaks to us, it has power to delight us, to add meaning to our rich life's journey. We should only have things in our home that are meaningful to us, memorable, even going back to our first recollections as a child.

Seeing a hand-blown pitcher reminds me of a trip to France almost thirty years ago when our daughters Alexandra and Brooke were very young. We brought this pitcher home after watching glass blowers at a factory in Biot, near Nice. All these years I've enjoyed using this treasured object for flowers, lemonade, or iced tea. Somehow this modest purchase on a family vacation awakens my memory to the entire experience, the way photographs and journals of that trip also keep the memory alive.

So many of my favorite things were found during our travels. I use a bed coverlet with embroidered pastel flowers that we purchased in Madeira, near Portugal, on another family holiday several years later. Making up the bed, using this pretty linen, sweetens my personal enjoyment of its beauty because of all the memories associated with the trip, including the memory of loving it the moment we saw it in the shop.

It takes a whole lot of living and celebrating life to acquire all the things we love and use. Our home tells our story, speaks without words about our interests, our family and friends, our travels, our hobbies and our passions. The more meaningful your possessions, the more pleasure you will experience when you spend precious time at home.

Our treasured things are daily reminders of our life's direction and focus so far. We keep our children's childhood drawings and letters. We love to use presents they've given us over the years—a glasses case, a set of placemats and napkins, cups and saucers, a scarf, a set of sheets, a vase, a wallet. We never seem to forget the provenance of a gift or of a purchase we felt spoke to us.

What are some of your favorite things? How do you connect to them? Why are they so significant? Look around your rooms. This is your life— your time alive. While on this earth in our body, we also have a larger body: a house we've made a home because of our love of what we put in it. Every day we all add to our life story. Most of the things we care about are not replaceable. They are not things bought in a mall, but manifestations of our character and personality. Some of my most sacred things are:

- ❋ Love letters
- ❋ My journals and notebooks
- ❋ My library of marked-up books that I've read, reread and studied
- ❋ Photographs of our children, friends and people we especially admire
- ❋ Objects we were given from our grandparents, parents, godparents, children and friends

❋ Scrapbooks
❋ Unpublished manuscripts
❋ Letters from friends and readers
❋ Letters from my spiritual mentor and my literary mentor
❋ Letters from my mother and brother just before they died
❋ Letters from Alexandra and Brooke
❋ A favorite gold pin that belonged to my best friend
   who died at age forty-four
❋ My slide library
❋ My photographs

Our home environment is very much alive. At home we see where we've been and our journey can continue to be adventurous and thrilling. We are living our life's story and our home tells the truth about these chapters of our happiness.

❋

LOOKING AT YOUR LIFE AND LIVING SPACES, YOU WILL SOON SEE THE
CONNECTION BETWEEN EACH ROOM, LIKE PARTS OF THE BODY,
AND WITH EACH ASPECT OF YOUR LIFE, LIKE PARTS OF YOUR SOUL.

WILLIAM SPEAR

CHAPTER THREE

Style

Create Your Individual
Style for Living

*I*n 1974, Doubleday published my first book, *Style for Living: How to Make Where You Live You.* I've always felt that our home is our larger self. The more we know ourselves and establish a sense of identity, the more we will be able to express what is unique in our personality.

As you create your individual style for living, you will see everything as one big whole where your sense of pleasure and happiness depends on fulfilling all the varied aspects of your life. Everything reveals who we are in our core. Our entire life is created by us, by our self-selected goals. Our deliberate choices, one after another, have a mysterious way of bringing everything that expresses our individuality together into the big picture of who we are.

In *Style for Living,* I asked my readers to look in their clothes closets for color inspiration. The colors we love and identify with should be worn as well as selected to use in our house decoration, just as we relate to certain furniture styles because of our fondness for a certain country and region. For example, I have a great love of Provence. Not only is my favorite artist from this beautiful part of the world, but my ideal decorating style is French Provincial. This style of living makes me feel most at home.

Think about your style for living in its entirety: how you choose to spend your time, how you want to express yourself through your work, how you dress, how you travel, how you celebrate with family and friends. To have style, you should have a point of view. Being opinionated about everything about your life will help you to integrate the various aspects of your life into a cohesive, intelligent master plan.

In the late seventies, I was struggling to express my point of view about living beautifully every day. Dr. René Dubos, a microbiologist and philosopher, told me to think clearly about what we as human beings all do every day. We eat, we sleep, and we bathe. We stand up, we sit down, and we lie down. How we do these things is expressed through our personal style of living. Let everything that increases your love of your own life be clues to connect the dots between a tiny detail and how all the little things combine to form the strength and muscle of the whole.

I love the line in Frank Sinatra's song, "I did it my way." How many of us can say that with conviction? Recognize your own style for living by the things you love, the people you love, the places you love, and the work you love. Be proud you are different. Being eccentric is a sign that you are not somebody in the crowd, but you, longing to express your innate genius, to let your spirit free. Put your unique imprint on everything you do. Always look within in order to express your true essence.

There are four keys to help you create your individual style for living:

1 ❊ Choose happiness in your lifestyle
2 ❊ Live authentically
3 ❊ Live by the trinity of what is true, good and beautiful
4 ❊ Aspire to achieve authentic excellence

❊

WHEN FRIENDS ENTER A HOME, THEY SENSE ITS PERSONALITY AND CHARACTER, THE FAMILY'S STYLE OF LIVING—THESE ELEMENTS MAKE A HOUSE COME ALIVE WITH A SENSE OF IDENTITY, A SENSE OF ENERGY, ENTHUSIASM, AND WARMTH, DECLARING "THIS IS WHO WE ARE; THIS IS HOW WE LIVE."

RALPH LAUREN

Understatement Has Power

I n all artistic expression, restraint is an important discipline. When we simplify, we're able to amplify inner beauty and integrity. Look for the spirit within. Try to express yourself with clarity as you look for and express continuity.

When I plan a dinner menu, arrange flowers, pack for a trip, decorate a room or dress for a party, I try to be subtle. There is great impact and elegance in being straightforward. Repetition of elements is a good way to create quiet elegance. A white pitcher filled with yellow roses has great charm. Consider using just one fabric in one room, for curtains as well as upholstery. Your dinner table can have a simple color theme of blue and white that is crisp, fresh, and looks heavenly. Your bed can look great with lots of white pillows and some pretty flowered sheets.

I think the word *entertaining* intimidates many people into feeling that they have to be extravagant. Any form of excess is imbalanced. I, for example, rarely give dinner parties anymore; I prefer having suppers. Everyone feels more relaxed and a simple roasted chicken with a salad and some vegetables makes perfect sense.

I love to live and work simply, and so far I've resisted the efforts of others who want me to complicate my life and pull me away from my style of living.

I live deliberately in order to enjoy all aspects of life. Having a simple, clear style saves time, energy and money. There is less waste.

I consider my taste to be more handsome than cute. I've never felt comfortable with frills and fussy designs. When a woman has confidence, she can wear tailored clothes and her inner beauty shines forth. I love pretty clothes and enjoy looking well put together, but I never feel beautiful if the clothes overpower my self-expression. I prefer clothes that complement my personality. In decorating, I try to help create rooms that are backgrounds for the personalities in the family rather than trying to create drama in an empty room. The decoration is not the end goal; we should create spaces where we can celebrate our time alive most fully.

The artist Roger Mühl's painting style has great simplicity. No one can copy his unique work because they always add too much detail; they fuss up the canvas. Roger Mühl has learned limit and control; it is in what he leaves out of the canvas that gives the power of expression. Remember the message in the ancient temple of Delphi in Greece: "Nothing in excess." When we're able to simplify, we save our time to do what is most important to us every day. It is a gift to be simple, but we cultivate this through setting strict limits and moving away from overdoing, overstating, being too dramatic. Our power will shine through from within when we strive to be restrained in our outward expressions of our personal style. When we refine our emotions, we generally tend to simplify.

Have unwavering integrity, sincerity and simplicity. Create an ambiance that is vitally alive, comfortable, gracious and relaxed. Our inner personality always should inform our outward expressions. I want to live an unobtrusively beautiful life in my time alive.

❋

SIMPLICITY IS THE MOST DIFFICULT THING TO SECURE IN THIS WORLD;
IT IS THE LAST LIMIT OF EXPERIENCE AND THE LAST EFFORT OF GENIUS.

GEORGE SAND

27

It's Great to Be Graceful

ALL THAT IS IMPORTANT IS THIS ONE MOMENT IN MOVEMENT.
MAKE THE MOMENT VITAL AND WORTH LIVING. DON'T LET IT SLIP
AWAY UNNOTICED OR UNUSED.

MARTHA GRAHAM

I was a clumsy, awkward tomboy as a child. I enjoyed climbing trees, playing baseball with my brothers, and gardening. When my mother enrolled me in ballet class I did somersaults when it was my turn to do a solo performance. My parents put a tennis racquet in my hand and I immediately took to the game. I opened my eyes and body to the power of graceful movement.

When we free our bodies from inhibitions, freely dancing to the rhythms of the universe, we feel the energies of the gods; we feel free, radiantly alive. Free movement is all. When we are happy, our bodies are truly wondrous to behold. Nothing is more wonderful than our human body when our spirit is pure joy, pure light, pure love. Our spirits soar as our energies release powerful messages to our bodies that can make us feel ecstatic. We should understand the significance of freely moving our bodies. Being uptight is bad for our health and limits our spontaneous enjoyment of the present moment's unlimited opportunities. When we're in the swing, in the flow of life, we want to dance for joy, skip and reach out to others with outstretched arms.

We always love ourselves more when we move our bodies freely, tenderly, openly. We show appreciation to others by our gracefulness exemplified through our tone of voice, our simple gestures, our generosity of spirit, our courtesy and thoughtfulness. When we are graceful, we are elegant and have a pleasing quality about us. We move with seemingly effortless beauty. We are reinforced by the accompanying joy.

To improve your gracefulness, consider signing up for a series of dance classes, take up yoga, do stretches every morning. All of us can improve our carriage. I wear ballet slippers at home and wherever I go, and I've grown to enjoy dancing around the house whether music is playing or not. We're supposed to take ten thousand steps a day in order to stay fit and healthy. Why not enjoy every single one? When we move well, we're vitally alive. Step, step.

❋

'I FEEL MY LIMBS ARE MADE GLORIOUS BY
THE TOUCH OF THIS WORLD OF LIFE.

RABINDRANATH TAGORE

28

Luxuries Matter

GIVE US THE LUXURIES OF LIFE, AND WE WILL DISPENSE
WITH ITS NECESSITIES.

OLIVER WENDELL HOLMES

I'm fond of sumptuous indulgences—a sip of good champagne to toast the bride and groom, a spray of a favorite French perfume, a totally free day with no appointments, a delicious meal prepared by a great chef, a Thai massage, a romantic evening at home for two. I don't suffer from guilt when I luxuriate because life is so rich with opportunities that provide us with pleasure and comfort. To deny ourselves some indulgences is to turn our back on the very things that we appreciate and that offer us tastes of luxury we do not depend on or expect as the focus of our lives.

If someone gives you a ride in his or her limousine, this is a real luxury you enjoy, knowing full well it is not a necessity. A luxury to you might be a simple, small wedding with only close family and friends, without any extravagances, expensive caviar and other costly frills. The luxury is in having this celebration the way you'll feel the happiest. A luxurious wedding doesn't necessarily mean that it is costly or grand.

I love to luxuriate in a bubble bath, indulging myself in a few moments of ablutions when I'm in a spa tub of hot water, enjoying the relaxation completely. Some people don't take baths because a shower is quicker. I soak in a hot tub because I want to savor a sensuous experience in the privacy of my own bathroom. I often light a candle, I bring in flowers, play favorite music and daydream.

There are some luxuries I indulge in that are expensive and often hard to obtain. Black truffles immediately come to mind. The smell is mysterious, the experience is exotic, and I've been known to crave them off-season. When they're available, I treat myself to a truffle dish or two.

The key to the discussion of luxuries is to learn the difference between what gives you pleasure that is sumptuous, and what is necessity. Truffles are not necessary to my sense of celebration, my well-being, or my happiness. They are over-the-top luxuries. A dab of a favorite perfume is a grace note—not an excessive luxury, and certainly not a necessity, but I like to wear a little perfume. I consider a comfortable reading chair a necessity.

We are frugal in some areas of our lives in order to be able to indulge our pleasures in others. What are some ways you like to save money? What have you chosen not to indulge in? What are some luxuries you feel comfortable accepting, saying yes to? We do without hesitation what brings us pleasure. When it comes to what pleases us most, we are not hypocrites: I believe that every luxury I incorporate into my life—and there are a lot—is nonessential, but precious and a great privilege, and I'm grateful for all of them.

None of the luxuries that genuinely add to our pleasure are bad for us if we indulge in moderation. Give thanks for each one. Now is our time alive to accept the truth that luxuries matter. When they feel right, they are right. Whether you read in a hammock, go to Starbucks for an iced coffee on your dog walk, or go to a concert or ballet or museum, who is going to deny you these luxuries? Make a list of some of your favorite luxuries and enjoy checking off the ones you choose to make possible. Have one luxury a day. Life is too short not to.

Are you extravagantly crazy about luxury? I confess I am. I believe we should live in beautiful surroundings in our time alive. Is beauty a luxury or a necessity? You decide.

❀

PEOPLE HAVE DECLAIMED AGAINST LUXURY FOR TWO THOUSAND YEARS,
IN VERSE AND IN PROSE, AND PEOPLE HAVE ALWAYS DELIGHTED IN IT.

VOLTAIRE

29

See Yourself Coming and Going

CHEERFULNESS AND CONTENTMENT ARE GREAT
BEAUTIFIERS AND FAMOUS PRESERVERS OF GOOD LOOKS.

CHARLES DICKENS

*W*hen I had a media coach train me to be on television, I was videotaped from every angle. I remember how painful it was to see these tapes played back to me so I could see how I looked to the audience. Fortunately, I was able to correct most of my awkwardness before appearing on live television. I can laugh about it now, but it was distressing to see how silly I looked in my outfit with a sash that tied in the back. When I moved around the set, demonstrating interior design ideas, I looked ridiculous—a bow in the back looks adorable on a little girl, not on me.

All too often we look at ourselves in a mirror and we see only our fronts. Peter and I have side-by-side closets with full-length mirrors on the inside of the doors so I can look at myself front, back and profile. I also have a mirror in the back of my closet because my clothes hang on one side, front to back, and I have built-in drawers on the opposite wall, so I can see myself from all sides in the mirrors, and can dress appropriately.

When I try on clothes in a store, the dressing room often has a triple mirror with the two side wings on hinges. We deserve to know how we look to others. If you're a member of a wedding, for example, people's main impression of you is from the back. When we have our hair cut or styled, the hairdresser hands us a mirror so we can see our hair from the back.

At home in the privacy of your bedroom or dressing area, take a look at yourself naked. I always suck in my stomach before I do, but people see us front, back and sides when we're not holding in our stomachs. Our figure is not set in stone. Our weight fluctuates and gets distributed in different parts of our body.

Looking in a full-length mirror naked and dressed is telling. Many people love themselves no matter what they weigh. We all come in different shapes and sizes. How much we weigh is not as important as how well we feel, how well we eat and how active we are.

Take a good look in the mirror—I know it can be shocking! Take stock and do what is in your best interest. Find the balance between accepting who you are and challenging yourself to change what you can.

❀

IT IS NO USE TO BLAME THE LOOKING GLASS IF YOUR FACE IS AWRY.

NIKOLAI GOGOL

You've Gotta Have a Look

*W*hatever your shape and size, you can flatter your body by your personal style of clothing. Some things you can change and others you cannot. Bones are bones. What you choose to wear is up to you. Coco Chanel believed old clothes are old friends, and this is certainly true. But our style is continuously evolving and the way we want to feel and look changes over time.

As we mature, we tend to feel more comfortable with who we are and with being ourselves; expressing ourselves honestly is terribly important. No matter where I am or who I am with, I always want to feel comfortable with myself.

Style permeates our whole persona because it is our life force expressing itself. Dare to be true to yourself. Fully appreciate who you are as you deliberately build on your dreams.

I've always been a fan of Katharine Hepburn. She had pluck and was never afraid to be herself. In the 1950s when she and Spencer Tracy stayed at Claridges in London, she was constantly reprimanded for wearing trousers—her signature trademark. Rather than changing her style, she used the staff entrance. Style means lifestyle. You choose the clothes that are suitable for your life. Many icons in the fashion world have formulas that work for them. They wear a uniform of sorts because they have found what suits them.

Thanks to the American designer Halston, in the 1960s, women were introduced to the well-designed pantsuit. Some women don't have the figure to wear pants and look put together, but many do and look wonderful. Jackie Kennedy maintained her great physique until her death at sixty-eight. While she had a large wardrobe of beautiful clothes, she looked smashing in blue jeans and a T-shirt.

We have a choice. We can either be self-confident or self-conscious. Some of the designer clothes that get copied for the masses are absurd. Too few fashion designers know that real women have breasts. Blouses and shirts are cut so straight that front buttons often gape, exposing a bra. Be careful to select clothing styles that are flattering to *your* body.

My friend and literary agent, Carl Brandt, raved about the lead actress Zoe Caldwell who played the opera singer Maria Callas in a triumphant performance in the Broadway play *Master Class*. I immediately bought tickets to see it, and Peter and I made an after-dinner reservation at one of our favorite restaurants, Café des Artistes. This promised to be a special evening. I got dressed up. We don't get all dressed up all that often, so there was excitement in the air. I wore a hot fuchsia, Thai silk, sleeveless sheath dress with a matching fitted coat. I felt elegant when we left the apartment for a fun evening on the town. The play was electrifying from the moment the actress took center stage. I, frankly, was spellbound. When, as Callas, she told the audience, "You've gotta have a look," I laughed so hard I was in tears. We ended up going back two more times, sitting once way up in the balcony with our daughter Brooke, who also broke into gales of laughter at this line.

You've gotta have a look. A room has got to have a look. The great truth is the look you've "gotta have" has to be yours and yours alone. No one else knows how you feel. No one else can express your unique style. Be patient with yourself. The clearer you are about who you are in your essence, the more fun it will be for you to put together your look. Try to focus on your body and your personality, not on clothes you admire on someone else.

Learn to avoid mistakes such as purchasing a pair of slacks that are too tight and too short because you love the color or design. Once you know that Capri pants make you look as though you outgrew them, you'll never be tempted to buy a pair again. You will make mistakes, but try to register each one and be strict with yourself to say no to anything that isn't the most flattering to your body. I love Capri pants; they don't love me. I look best in pants that are ankle length.

Regularly spend time trying on the clothes in your closet and give away or bring to a local thrift shop those that no longer flatter you. There will never be enough time to waste wearing clothes that are dull, that don't fit you well or, worse, that you know are not your "look." Onward and upward. There isn't a dress rehearsal for your time alive. You are center stage. You are the star of your show. You've gotta have a look. The time is now while you have a body and can wear attractive clothes that express your spirit.

❊

ZEST IS THE SECRET OF ALL BEAUTY.
THERE IS NO BEAUTY THAT IS ATTRACTIVE WITHOUT ZEST.

CHRISTIAN DIOR

31

Beware of Advertisements

HE WHO KNOWS HE HAS ENOUGH IS RICH.

TAO TE CHING

*T*elevision, newspapers and magazines need advertisers to support their revenue. While some ads are accurate and the product is of real value when purchased and used, there are a great many products that are a complete waste of our time and money.

Before you get caught up in something that is advertised, first think about what you want or need, not what is available. So much of ad copy is meant to intimidate you, to make you feel unhappy with who you are—to convince you that without a facelift or some miracle wrinkle cream, you will look awful as you age.

I'm embarrassed to think of the money I've wasted buying products I became brainwashed into needing. The cosmetics industry knows that society likes women to remain eternally youthful, to have skin that is wrinkle free. Each product is expensive and our dermatologists often advise us to throw them all out. As we age, often our skin becomes more sensitive, so we should consult our skin doctor before going to a department store cosmetics counter and purchasing products that the cosmetician feels are best for us.

There is a great deal of information out there. We're bombarded with offers at every turn. Everything looks so glamorous, so useful, so time saving, and so important in the ads. But who pays? What is the true value when you consider the cost? Will a product improve the quality of your life? Do you believe the product is good for you? *Fat free* doesn't mean *non-fattening*. Cereals that add the crunch may also add sugar.

As an exercise, look through your daily newspaper, reading the ads as well as the news. Do the same with the magazines you read. Watch television one evening, paying attention to the commercials. Have you noticed how fast-talking the television commercial announcer is at the end of the ad? Can you really read the fine print—understand the side effects, the disclaimers?

Rather than feeling hopelessly inadequate because you don't have a new automobile or a huge estate or some expensive watch, take heart. Be grateful your needs are few. His Holiness the Dalai Lama teaches us to give up our attachments. We're human and divine. We will always have desires, and our wants will never be fully satisfied, but we can curb our appetite for things that will not contribute to our well-being. "The more you know, the less you need," a wise Australian Aboriginal saying suggests. Celebrate all the things you don't want or need. Spend your time being a free spirit who is happy now, just as you are, without any more stuff to pay for and maintain.

❋

HOW MANY THINGS I CAN DO WITHOUT.

SOCRATES

32

Let Go of What Was Once Wonderful

SEEK OUT THAT PARTICULAR MENTAL ATTITUDE WHICH MAKES YOU FEEL
MOST DEEPLY AND VITALLY ALIVE, ALONG WITH WHICH COMES THE INNER
VOICE WHICH SAYS, "THIS IS THE REAL ME," AND WHEN YOU HAVE FOUND
THAT ATTITUDE, FOLLOW IT.

WILLIAM JAMES

*W*hat are some of the things you did in your past that you loved to do that you are no longer able to do? When it became apparent I could no longer play tennis, I accepted it, filling in the time reading and writing.

In our remaining time, we are the ones who fill our cup so it is brimming with zest, with new challenges, new opportunities to grow, to learn, and to feel greater vitality and more limitless joy. I've cultivated the habit of not pining for what is not right for me now. I can't do everything, but I can do many things. I take pleasure in my specific life. I accept my age, my figure, and my health issues. I don't fight against the aging process because it is inevitable. Accepting what is the truth makes life easier and better. We mature and our bodies change. Truth can't be changed. I'm a student of truth—it always is here with us, guiding us, informing us, showing us what we should do, what we should not do and what we should stop doing.

I can remember whizzing around the sidewalks of New York City in tightly fitted sleeveless sheath dresses with a deep tan, blond hair tossing in the air. Ah, those were the days. Ah no, *these* are the days! I lived each day fully and, looking back, appropriately. Now I'm living a new chapter. I still expose my bare arms occasionally, but they are not a rich nutty brown color, nor do they look the way they did when I was playing tennis all day and swimming and running after two rambunctious little girls. Now, I wear long sleeves when I want to look elegant. My childhood hair was spun silk the color of buttered corn on the cob. My blond hair of adulthood was helped with chemicals at the hairdressers. Now alas, my hair is light brown salted with gray.

One in four women dyes her hair. I no longer can because I am allergic to any chemical put on my scalp. My dermatologist told me that it would be dangerous to continue to try to hide the gray hair. Taking even a slight chance that I would die one day earlier because of dying my hair is not an option. I value every second of my time alive. I accept my natural highlights and am often complimented on them. How is it possible to be a ninety-year-old blonde and have a face that is compatible? My mother had dark brown hair and dyed it regularly. Toward the end of her life in her sixties, she let it go naturally gray and her face looked more beautiful.

I've consulted many expert back and foot doctors and have been told unanimously that I should wear flat shoes with no heel. I obey my doctors because they make sense. They're telling me the truth. I got rid of more than a dozen pairs of pretty high-heeled shoes. I loved my shoes, but I look back and realize that they contributed to my back troubles; I acquired bunions and my feet hurt when I walked.

Style should look effortless and be comfortable. My personal evolution brings me to wearing my colorful signature ballet slippers. I have them in every color imaginable. They are so comfortable; it is as though I'm walking on air. I put innersoles inside for more cushion. Ah, to be so happy, in the swing of life, whooshing around on pain-free feet. How many people claim such a luxury?

I'm far more interested in who I'm becoming than how I used to look, how I used to be. We grow old when we stop having fun, when we stop doing things we love to do, when we do things in order to fit in. I don't want to fit in. I want to stand out. I want to be the best me that I can be.

What do you want to let go of that was once wonderful? Perhaps it is red meat, hard liquor, wearing suits, smoking, sleeping on ironed sheets, your car, unhealthy desserts, out-of-date clothes, fur coats, unsuitable relationships, tennis, weekly pedicures, sugar and cream in your coffee, constant television, or unused jewelry. We don't choose the truth; the truth chooses us. Think clearly about your sublime time alive—how to spend it, how to enjoy and celebrate it. When we close one door, we open another. Not the same door, but one that will bring us great hope and new opportunities. Now that I have grandchildren, I can wear ballet slippers that are the same colors as Anna's and Lily's. How grand is that!

✻

THE CURIOUS PARADOX IS THAT WHEN 1 ACCEPT MYSELF JUST AS 1 AM,
THEN 1 CAN CHANGE.

CARL ROGERS

33

You Are Your Best Color Expert

THE PUREST AND MOST THOUGHTFUL MINDS ARE THOSE
WHICH LOVE COLOR THE MOST.

JOHN RUSKIN

*T*he colors we wear, the colors we surround ourselves with, have energy. The clearer the color, the more wavelengths of energy. Color *is* energy. Of all the things that an interior designer does, the most essential contribution is to help clients establish their color palette. The colors we love should be consistently used in every area of our lives.

I am an unabashedly over-the-top lover of clear colors from nature. Since my earliest childhood memory is of being surrounded by color in a garden, paradise for me is always being around flowers. I love the awesome beauty of all flowers, all shades, tones and varieties. I love to look at the sky, at turquoise and cobalt blue water, at fresh spring green grass, at flowering fruit trees and at the riot of colors of vegetables.

We eat color, we drink color, we wear color and we choose the colors in our environment—indoors and in the garden. I recognize white as a color. I prefer bright, clear white. I choose brilliant white paper to write on, I select the whitest fax paper available, and I choose the whitest exterior house paint—and then add a touch of blue.

I want clarity and purity. Light is white. White is light. Clean, fresh white makes us smile, gives us energy and a sense of serenity. Seeing puffy clouds in a blue sky makes me happy. White expands space. A pure white room looks twice as large as a dark, dreary paneled room. I enjoy wearing white, although I'm aware that it enlarges the figure as well as a space.

Have you established your color palette? Has your passion for certain colors faded and you've made new discoveries? I ask friends what color glass or ribbon they want and their answers are so spontaneous: "Yellow. I need more yellow in my life." Or, "Blue, I love blue." What are the colors that bring you the most joy? What are the color combinations that you most love? What are some colors that you don't like? I like orange in food, and I wear orange, but I don't like it in flower bouquets.

There are so many fresh, clear, wonderful colors available in everything imaginable; we have no excuse to be dreary. Open your closet, open your drawers, what do you see? People tease me, but I won't change; I'll only get more excited about color. I go to stores hunting for color in ink, paper clips and even rubber bands. The brand of rubber bands called "Brites" offers pink, orange, yellow, green, blue and violet. The copy on the package reads: "Sizzle without snap. Brites! Rubber bands add sunshine to your day while they help you do your job." Why put up with beige!

Pay no attention to so-called experts who tell you what colors you should wear and what colors you should avoid wearing. The colors you adore will make you look and feel the best. We always look great when we're happy, and there are certain colors that we enjoy wrapping ourselves up in. Through increasing our awareness of color we awaken to who we are. We're able to associate the colors we love with nature. We're alert to all experiences we've had where we've enjoyed specific colors and combinations.

Beware of drab colors being touted as great. If you enjoy a neutral color palette, be open to adding some green and a touch of red. If you find you don't feel right when you wear a certain color, don't force yourself to live with your mistake. Off to the thrift store again.

I'm a cheerleader for color because we can literally change our life—our mind, our attitude, our perspective and our whole point of view—when we are aware of the magical, mysterious power color has for us. Colors express and restore us, and they heal us. I let the spirit move me when I choose what color to wear. I feel sad that our Western tradition frowns on wearing bright colors at funerals. This is a time to remember the life of the person who has died and we can celebrate this positive energy through color.

I feel energized and restored when I wear certain favorite colors: hot fuchsia pink and bright apple green have a magic ability to lift my spirits. Getting dressed I feel the great energy of the positive association I experience when I wear these colors—even in the sad times.

I'm a happy colorist. I think this universal splendor of color, given to us at no extra cost, is a treasured gift. Lack of color is sensory deprivation. The creator of the character Zorba the Greek, Nikos Kazantzakis, gives us this message: "If you don't like your life, change it. You are the artist. You have the canvas, brushes, and colors." Paint heaven and in you go.

Add more touches of color to your life and watch your vital energy, your ch'i, increase. We live in this magnificent world that is perfectly wondrous in its rainbow of refreshing colors. They're ours if we accept them. All we have to do is say yes to the invitation to color our lives in nature's beauty.

Consider a few of the things in your life where you can add favorite colors: glassware, placemats, erasers, scissors, towels, pillows, eyeglasses, straws, pots and pans, flower vases, bottles, stationery, notepaper, postcards, ink, pens, mechanical pencils, envelopes, sheets, countertops, scarves, socks, shirts, slacks, watchbands, belts, shoes, napkins, tablecloths, jewelry, rugs, our ironing board cover, wrapping paper, ribbons, tote bags, candles, jackets, underpants, bras, soaps, neckties, the patio umbrella, chair cushions, flowering plants, fresh-cut flowers, photo frames, dog collars, curtains, clipboards, cups and saucers, stamps, doors, room colors, flatware handles, tacks, storage boxes, artwork, quilts, plates, hardware. Add your own!

❀

JUST TO PAINT IS GREAT FUN. THE COLOURS ARE LOVELY TO LOOK AT AND DELICIOUS TO SQUEEZE OUT. MATCHING THEM, HOWEVER CRUDELY, WITH WHAT YOU SEE IS FASCINATING AND ABSOLUTELY ABSORBING. TRY IT IF YOU HAVE NOT DONE SO—BEFORE YOU DIE.

SIR WINSTON CHURCHILL

34

Eat Beautifully

STRANGE TO SEE HOW A GOOD DINNER AND
FEASTING RECONCILES EVERYBODY.

SAMUEL PEPYS

*E*veryone who knows me understands my passion for good, fresh food. I have a healthy appetite and love to say jokingly that I've never missed a meal. Darn few, to be sure. Food is one of my ten defining words that I wrote about in *Feeling at Home* and *Choosing Happiness*.

I believe sitting down to an attractively set table with fresh flowers and the anticipation of a pleasurable meal and stimulating conversation is one of life's greatest gifts. I love to eat beautifully whether I am alone or with family and friends. Eating beautifully benefits everyone. When we savor a good meal, we are nourishing our soul as we fuel our body. We will only be able to eat food and drink nectars while we're alive. Good food is not only healthy, but we become more enthusiastic, more excited, about our daily life when we sit down to a proper, attractive meal.

Whether we prepare and cook dinner at home or go out to a restaurant, the experience should be one of celebration. Every act we do should be a loving one. Eating beautifully is an excellent use of your sacred time alive. Even if you are alone, come to the ceremony of eating with a sense of grace and appreciation, ready to communicate with your heart. There is no sense of rushing when we treat this important ritual with reverence.

Before I begin to eat, I think of all the people who contributed to the food availability and I'm thankful. I think of loved ones not "at table" and I bless them. If I am alone, I light a candle no matter what the time of day. If I am with others, I begin in a number of ways—by holding hands and squeezing those on either side of me, or simply by raising my glass and making eye contact and giving a toast.

I'm a great admirer of Julia Child. Many years ago we were both teaching different subjects at the University of Cannes in the South of France. Peter, Julia Child and I spent the better part of three days together. She was affable and seemed to enjoy our company. We'd go to classes with her when we were not teaching our own. At the end of the Young Presidents Organization's international conference, we were all bused to Monaco to a black-tie dinner party. After the cocktail reception, we were happy Julia chose to join us at our table. I told her of the years when I was a young bride whose mother-in-law was a great cook. I had to pull myself together and learn how; I used Julia's book *Mastering the Art of French Cooking* as my bible. I demonstrated how she gave me the courage to flip an omelet in a Teflon pan, make beef Bourguignon and veal chasseur from scratch, and told her my favorite signature dish is her recipe for leg of lamb with a mustard espresso paste, garlic and pan-roasted Spanish olives.

Julia Child maintained her passion for life right to the end. She was the ultimate *bonne vivante*. Whenever she was asked what her guilty pleasures were, she'd respond, "I don't have any." Here's a woman who owned and used eight hundred knives, and believed that we could change the world. I agree completely with her advice: "Eat everything. Have fun. French cooking is the most important in the world, one of the few that has rules. If you follow the rules, you can cook pretty well."

Julia Child was my teacher in learning to be fearless about food. I'm forever her student. Let's toast Julia Child who found her passion, who lived her life pursuing everything positive and who exuded joy in her time alive.

Eat beautifully. Our meals are our daily celebrations, urging us to suck the marrow of the bone, to live beautifully in gratitude for life's bounty, and to love the life we choose to live.

❋

THE DISCOVERY OF A NEW DISH DOES MORE FOR HUMAN HAPPINESS
THAN THE DISCOVERY OF A NEW STAR.

ANTHELME BRILLAT-SAVARIN

CHAPTER FOUR

Enthusiasm

35

What Excites You Defines You

"JUST LIVING IS NOT ENOUGH," SAID THE BUTTERFLY.
"ONE MUST HAVE SUNSHINE, FREEDOM, AND A LITTLE FLOWER."

HANS CHRISTIAN ANDERSEN

The more things that excite you, the more intensely you will live your time alive. Whenever we're emotionally engaged, we're more focused, more alert, more aware. Our lives are defined more by our actions than by our words. Intuitively, we secretly know who we are and how we should live. The key is to trust this inner guidance and believe we are the only one who can figure it out. Because there is no one else in the world like us, it is our job to follow our unique path. When we do, we experience joy.

What are you most interested in? What would you love to be doing more of? Do you love to travel to exotic far-off places? Do you love good food and go distances to eat in restaurants with a reputation for excellence? Do you get excited about going to the opera or do you prefer the ballet? Are you more interested in tennis or golf or would you rather go hiking? Do you get excited when you have the time to prepare a beautiful dinner for your children?

I get stirred up at the littlest things: listening to a favorite song, wearing a cheerful color, seeing new buds and blossoms on the rose bushes, going to the farmers' market, hanging out at a coffee shop with a friend. When we're vitally alive, enthusiastic about all our varied interests, life takes on a whole new meaning. I love being at an elevated energy level that motivates me to touch up some woodwork with white paint or study philosophy.

Too often people become so bogged down in responsibilities and duties that they put aside their own interests. It's important to keep our excitement alive in a wide range of interests that evoke a mental state that is arousing and holds our attention. What do you love to do that is so absorbing that you lose all sense of time? Do you love to sail? What kinds of books do you love to read? What are you most curious about? Now is the time to go to a concert in the park or go to the theater. I get excited when I write a note to a friend or wrap a present to give a child or grandchild. I feel all of life can be an exciting adventure to be lived exuberantly.

William Blake understood that energy is eternal delight. I have enthusiasm for so many different things, sometimes I don't know what to do next. I hunger to keep this sense of excitement alive. Whenever we are interested in a lot of different things, we energize others who come in contact with us. Energy is contagious.

We are defined by all that we love, all that we find beautiful. A three-year-old daughter of a friend jumps for joy and says, "I'm so 'cited." It doesn't take much to be " 'cited." Trust your intuition to know what's exciting the same way an innocent child does.

❋

THE SAME STREAM OF LIFE THAT RUNS THROUGH MY VEINS NIGHT AND DAY RUNS THROUGH THE WORLD AND DANCES IN RHYTHMIC MEASURES.

RABINDRANATH TAGORE

36

All Play Requires Practice, Practice, Practice

FOR THE THINGS WE HAVE TO LEARN BEFORE WE CAN DO THEM,
WE LEARN BY DOING THEM.

WE ARE WHAT WE REPEATEDLY DO. EXCELLENCE, THEN,
IS NOT AN ACT, BUT A HABIT.

ARISTOTLE

*M*y definition of play includes all of life's work, whatever job is before us. I believe we should all work at play. Luck tends to come to the prepared soul. Except when we're sleeping, every aspect of our life requires focused effort. How we direct our energies adds up to how well we live our lives. We continuously use physical and mental energy in order to accomplish the task at hand. I believe the activities we engage in should be constructive, not destructive, and they should be as enjoyable as humanly possible.

Mihaly Csikszentmihalyi, the writer and teacher who has devoted decades of research on the happiness we derive from being in a state of flow, believes emphatically, "It is essential to *learn to enjoy life*. It really does not make sense to go through the motions of existence if one doesn't appreciate as much of it as possible."

In our time alive, we want to be useful, to give back, not to merely live, but to thrive, to live well. I can't imagine waking up in the morning and dreading what I had to do all day. Many people have a job as a necessary occupation to sustain themselves and survive. But when we don't like what we're doing, life becomes stale, even unbearable. When we feel our work is drudgery, we die a little every day. Our light, our energy, our power, leave us; we feel heavy, even depressed. But there is no drudgery or monotonous job or task for someone who has cultivated the right attitude. Everyone has responsibilities. It matters what we do to carve out a beautiful life for ourselves. Most of us work extremely hard. When we find pleasure in our direct experience with process, we are blessed. This job that is before us is ours to do well. We do our best whatever we do because that is what we're called to do. We're meant to give our all to life. When we play, we occupy ourselves in amusement, in a sport or some other kind of recreation. We enter into an activity with the intention of enjoying ourselves. We appreciate our life and take part in it energetically.

The harder I work and play, the greater my satisfaction in the present moment, as well as my eventual accomplishment. When we practice, practice, practice, we become good at what we do. We perfect our skills with repeated exercise. With practice we can become proficient at our chosen occupation. Someone who does public speaking gets better the more he or she does it. The best speakers are inspiring because they love what they're doing. They lift us out of our complacency and point our lives upward above mediocrity.

Being good at what we do brings more life force to us. We draw more and more from life the more we give of ourselves to life. You give your all because this is who you are. You don't practice to earn a living. You practice to have a great life, to express the best, the wisest, and the most beautiful that is in you.

I cannot imagine a worse curse than boredom. I love to work playfully and to practice playing. I enjoy making an effort for joy. I find that the variety of opportunities for me to express my love of life is limitless. Things that activate my mind train my mind. Because of this truth, I enjoy being alone to think things through with no interruptions. Equally, I enjoy the sizzle and pop of being with a friend. What a thrill to strike up a conversation. I flirt with the interacting of all dimensions of life. Several of the doormen in my apartment building get a kick out of the colorful way I dress. Once complimented, I skip, giving them a charge as I get a charge.

If I'm on a groove window shopping and end up in a favorite card store, I invariably buy a couple of cards or a box of enticing stationery because I love having pretty paper to spread love around. Colorful notecards, postcards and stationery inspire me to spontaneously write a note to a loved one.

When we get out of the way and directly connect to the moment, we appreciate the task at hand. We can use our minds, our hearts, our souls, and our hands to bring something out of ourselves that is good and useful. There is joy right here.

When we're able to occupy ourselves in pleasing ways, we often smile, laugh and discover things about ourselves we didn't know before. Learn to like whatever you do. Let practice be a daily habit. When we cultivate habits of mind and character that bring out the best that is in us, our time alive will shine brilliantly. Whether we practice the piano, a dance step, our handwriting, playing golf, tennis, acting, writing, or singing, in order to polish our skills, we need to practice, practice, practice.

What are some of your interests that you want to improve upon? What do you want to bring forth that is uniquely you? Learn from doing.

❀

IF THERE IS SOMETHING GREAT IN YOU, IT WILL NOT APPEAR
ON YOUR FIRST CALL. IT WILL NOT APPEAR AND COME TO YOU EASILY,
WITHOUT ANY WORK AND EFFORT.

EMERSON

37

A God Within

'EVERYTHING IS DETERMINED, THE BEGINNING AS WELL AS THE END, BY
FORCES OVER WHICH WE HAVE NO CONTROL. 'IT IS DETERMINED FOR THE
INSECT AS WELL AS FOR THE STAR. 'HUMAN BEINGS, VEGETABLES OR COSMIC
DUST, WE ALL DANCE TO A MYSTERIOUS TUNE, INTONED IN THE DISTANCE
BY AN INVISIBLE PLAYER.

ALBERT EINSTEIN

*I*n the fall of 1972, I was at a spiritual service at Lincoln Center on a sunny, crisp autumn day. The minister spoke of a new book he'd read and recommended it to the audience. The book, *The God Within: A Positive Philosophy for a More Complete Fulfillment of Human Potentials,* was written by Dr. René Dubos. The message of this book has been life-transforming for me, coloring my perception and my philosophy.

In his opening chapter, "The Hidden Aspects of Reality," Dr. Dubos writes:

> *The pre-classical and classical Greeks symbolized the hidden aspects*
> *of man's nature, in particular the forces that motivate him to perform*
> *memorable deeds by the entheos—a god within. From "entheos"*
> *is derived "enthusiasm," one of the most beautiful words in any*
> *language. Man today may no longer believe in the divine origin*
> *of inspiration, but there are few who do not retain the ancient and*
> *almost mystical faith that enthusiasm is the source of creativity.*

What would life be like without our enthusiasms? Without this "divine madness"? Socrates and Plato believed our greatest blessing is sent to us as a gift of the gods. What is your source of inspiration?

When we experience enthusiasm, we feel a new kind of freedom that can profoundly change our personality. There is an awakening, a light that transcends our consciousness. This mysterious force is a god within. This gift is given to human beings, inspiring us to create a life of significance. Live and celebrate in appreciation of this motivating inner force, this effervescent blessing. Enthusiasm urges us onward and upward. Open, receptive, aware of the highest and finest within us, we "dance to a mysterious tune" that is uniquely ours.

❋

A PERSON, A PLACE, A FRAGMENT OF MATTER ARE THE MANIFESTATIONS OF INNER FORCES AND PATTERNS WHICH MAY REMAIN HIDDEN UNTIL UNMASKED, RELEASED OR DEVELOPED BY WILLED CREATIVE ACTS OR FORTUNATE CIRCUMSTANCES.

RENÉ DUBOS

Act On Your Enthusiasms

*T*he happiest people are the ones whose choice of actions brings them pleasure. When we love what we're doing, we're appreciating our life. When we rejoice in our immediate life, we're wisely using our time. If you love to sing, why not join a local church choir? If you love to dance, take a dance class. What is keeping you from acting on your enthusiasms?

The more people, places and things we love, the more enthusiastic we are about our daily life. We can't fake enthusiasm. When we are being our authentic selves, we will have an exuberant spirit. All our energy will be constructive.

Think of all the people you love. What names come immediately to mind? Who inspires you to greater appreciation for the gift of life? Where do you like to go to awaken your enthusiasms? For me, water always inspires my spirit to soar. I love to gaze on an ocean and see nothing but sky, birds, a few clouds, waves, and an occasional boat on the horizon. At the water's edge, I come to myself, with space as well as time to contemplate.

The fire, passion and energy of your enthusiasm should direct your life's journey. Enthusiasm is the fuel, the glory, and the power that lights the world. When we're enthusiastic, we're magnets to exciting experiences, fun times and meaningful accomplishments. I agree with Emerson that nothing great was ever achieved without enthusiasm.

Some of us were born enthusiastic and others were not. If your parents were somber and went through life fighting against reality, wanting what they couldn't have, wondering why life passed them by, this was a poor environment for a child's spirit. But it's never too late to accept the gift of enthusiasm that leads to joyful self-expression.

You can develop an enthusiastic attitude. You might not have an enormous talent for a specific activity, but you can develop interests—in poetry or birdwatching or faux finishing or astrology—and become enthusiastic about your discoveries in nature and in your human nature. Keep trying new activities until some of them click. Try belly dancing or tap dancing. Moving our bodies increases our vitality—so does laughing at ourselves. This is a beginning.

Loss of enthusiasm quickens the aging process because you lose your life force. Your cells and your immune system weaken. When we're not enjoying ourselves, we feel old and we age prematurely because life is no longer fun. Unhappiness diminishes our light, our power.

Discover objects of your affection. Become passionate about the things you choose to live with. Awaken your senses. Tenderly, lovingly, find more and more things that appeal to you—whether it is a table that inspires your muse or a certain place you like to go on a walk, or a painting you love to gaze at. Be aware of the power of tangible, physical objects you find beautiful and useful to elevate your spirit. When you understand that everything has an inner force, a hidden dimension, your enthusiasm can be increased and sustained throughout a long, happy, meaningful life.

❋

DEVELOP INTEREST IN LIFE AS YOU SEE IT; IN PEOPLE, THINGS, LITERATURE, MUSIC—THE WORLD IS SO RICH, SIMPLY THROBBING WITH RICH TREASURES, BEAUTIFUL SOULS AND INTERESTING PEOPLE.

HENRY MILLER

39

Keep Your Flame Alive

JOY IS THE HOLY FIRE THAT KEEPS OUR PURPOSE WARM
AND OUR INTELLIGENCE AGLOW.

HELEN KELLER

*L*ife should never become dull. In order to express the best that's in us, we have to have fire in our belly. From my own experience and from observing my creative friends, I've learned that this fire should never be allowed to go out. This pure flame, this invisible light within us, needs to be constantly nourished. It's not automatic or easy. We nurture our enthusiasms in every action because we know how important it is. Because it is joy that brings forth our greatness.

Keeping the flame alive requires tremendous commitment. There is effort in taking up a new interest, in studying, in learning, in any form of original self-expression. Our life must be lived individually and expressed with conviction.

The more activities we love, the more we'll love life. As Aristotle taught us 2,500 years ago, "all men love more what they have won by labor." When we find things to be enthusiastic about, we fan the flame of enthusiasm. The more we put into life, the more we receive. My experience has persuaded me that the essential element of achieving our goals is steady perseverance (at enthusiasms!).

Go to rehearsal every week. Maybe the dishes won't get done until morning, but don't get stuck. You have to throw your energy into stimulating activities that extend you. If you keep going to classes or regular meetings you enjoy that are good for you and others, you will manage to keep the flame alive right to the end.

Make appointments with yourself. Write these entries in ink in your calendar. Keep these appointments as personal commitments. I know a writer who kept the flame alive by going to live in Bali six months of the year. Karen has such passion for the culture, the people, their philosophy and their beliefs that she dared to make this bold choice to redirect her life toward her enthusiasm.

You keep your flame alive by showing up, starting new activities, as well as continuing long-held ones. In the face of time pressures, difficulties and setbacks, whenever you're enthusiastic about learning something new, focus your energy on what you want. When I sincerely do this, I've found that the universe responds.

Take heart. You can't be in two places at one time. It is your responsibility to keep your enthusiasms alive. We gain our excitement from plunging into new exciting activities. Embrace the adventure. It might bring great joy to your life.

We don't fatigue when we are exhilarated, when we do whatever we're doing with our whole heart. All activities will increase our vitality. Force yourself to try new adventures, explore different techniques, and expose yourself to as much culture and beauty as possible. Your flame should and can burn brightly. Let this flame be your constant companion.

Strike up a conversation with the flight attendant or taxi driver. I'm always fascinated to learn how interesting people are. One taxi driver and I were talking about our favorite cities all over the world. I learned he was an opera singer who sang in all these countries. Peter and I have a favorite train conductor. Whenever we see Mike, we always enjoy catching up with his life. We know a porter who loves to play ice hockey. He's in his late sixties and plays in an adult league. Paul's face lights up when someone in the train station is carrying a hockey stick.

Don't be afraid to indulge yourself in the countless thousands of ways to keep your flame alive. You don't find extra time; you seize the time you have by letting go of things you are no longer passionate about. Continuously weed out the things in your life you are no longer passionate about or you choose not to make time for. Make a list. Draw a vertical line down the middle of a piece of paper. Label the left side "Things I want to do more of," and label the right side "Things I choose to do less of." For example, on my list I put "read more" on the left side and "watch less television" on the right side.

❋

NO ONE KEEPS UP HIS ENTHUSIASM AUTOMATICALLY. ENTHUSIASM
MUST BE NOURISHED WITH NEW ACTIONS, NEW ASPIRATIONS, NEW EFFORTS,
NEW VISION. COMPETE WITH YOURSELF; SET YOUR TEETH AND DIVE INTO
THE JOB OF BREAKING YOUR OWN RECORD. IT IS ONE'S OWN FAULT IF HIS
ENTHUSIASM IS GONE; HE FAILED TO FEED IT.

PAPYRUS

40

Is Your Inner Dialogue Positive?

WHAT YOU DON'T EXPERIENCE POSITIVELY, YOU WILL
EXPERIENCE NEGATIVELY.

JOSEPH CAMPBELL

Whether you are negative or positive is determined by you, not by external circumstances. You choose how you program your thoughts. Any negative thought is going to have negative consequences. There's no bigger waste of our time than to tear down the moment with negative energy. When we experience positive time, we build our lives constructively. No one controls our minds except ourselves. Our thoughts color our energy and spirit. When we deliberately put good ideas in our minds, we're able to accept the unexpected, to make the most of what we face.

The mind is the seat of human consciousness: thought, memory, perception, will, imagination and emotion originate in the brain. When we train our minds to create healthy mental states, we can intelligently solve problems, reason abstractly and learn from experience because of our keener understanding and our wiser thinking. Learn to be more acutely aware of what your mind is thinking. Self-awareness is a necessary art and skill that requires rigorous disciplined concentration, resulting in a change of attitude and perspective. Do you feel self-assured? Do you feel a sense of acceptance? Is your life increasingly exciting to you from day to day?

Whenever I have a negative thought, I try to replace it immediately with something useful. Challenge yourself to stay centered and calm when your time is disrupted by things that are beyond your control. The more exciting your life, the more inconveniences you'll experience. It comes with the territory. I often experience last-minute tour changes or radio hosts who cancel in the eleventh hour or, worse, don't phone in for an interview. I try to breathe deeply and tell myself it wasn't meant to be. Rather than dwelling on what could have been that didn't manifest, I try to focus on rescheduling. I don't think of lost opportunity; I choose to think I have something to look forward to in the future. I try to learn from my emotions.

One Tuesday morning I was scheduled to go on a live national radio show that meant I couldn't attend my favorite yoga class. I'd made the value judgment that the exposure from the radio interview was more important than the pleasure of my class. When the host called to say he couldn't do the show because he felt dreadful with the flu, I hung up and had to hold back tears. I learned how important being in the presence of Diana, my inspiring teacher, is to me every week. I was able to attend an afternoon class with someone else. The woman who schedules my radio shows now knows how important this weekly date is to me, so she works around my favorite yoga class.

Peter and I were in Minneapolis in a snowstorm. When we arrived at the airport we discovered our flight to Chicago had been canceled. We were very calm because we didn't want to go to Chicago; we wanted to go home to New York. The connecting flight was less than half the price of a nonstop one. We travel a great deal and often have to be inconvenienced because of budget concerns. Tom, the American Airlines ticket agent, checked the computer record and saw that we'd flown nonstop from New York to Minneapolis the day before and arranged for us to fly home on Northwest Airlines on a nonstop flight that was leaving in two hours. We ended up in a fun airport restaurant savoring a delicious grilled chicken salad, smiling at our good fortune to be on the flight we'd wanted all along. By sitting in the exit row with an empty middle seat, we felt we were more comfortable than if we were in first class. Good fortune is in the air. We have to keep our energy positive so we're able to fully appreciate all the good that we attract in our life.

If you are seated on a bus that has stopped because of mechanical trouble and you know you will never make your appointment on time, see it as an opportunity to stay positive. That is an accomplishment, and in the larger picture possibly more useful than the appointment!

The entertainer Art Linkletter said that "life is full of overwhelming odds. You can't really eliminate the negatives, but you can diminish them." Negative energy, negative spirit, and negative perspective are not friends of enthusiasm. Negativity tends to discourage rather than encourage. Pessimistic people tend to be disagreeable, noticing only the negative: the pizza is soggy and cold, the toast is burned, the weather is never right, it's too windy, it's too humid. When someone is depressed, his or her depression snuffs out the life force, and enthusiasm vanishes as in quicksand.

No one can make you negative without your approval. Deal with life from the highest perspective. Protect your consciousness from lowering your optimism. The reason it is crucial to know that there is a silver lining in every cloud is because in striving to perceive it you will stretch yourself to greater understanding of the truth. We can change our minds in changing circumstances, even when we can't change reality.

A Buddhist friend laughingly says, "What is, is. What isn't, isn't." Why become sad that things aren't always perfect if you have no power over situations beyond your control? Our time alive moments can be as big as years when we keep a positive outlook, no matter what is going on all around us.

We're fortunate. We're blessed. Things could be worse. We can make our lives better and better. This is where we should focus in order to keep our enthusiasms burning in our soul.

❀

THE MIND IS ITS OWN PLACE, AND IN ITSELF CAN MAKE
A HEAVEN OF HELL, OR A HELL OF HEAVEN.

JOHN MILTON

Oh, the Blue Hydrangea!

I have such reverence for blue hydrangeas; no cathedral could ever be as beautiful to me. Blue hydrangeas evoke "sacred awe." Is it possible to inherit such a strong attachment? Alexandra and Brooke share this over-the-top passion. Our hearts pound when we're near them. We are all goo-goo about blue hydrangeas.

The color we especially crave is Nikko blue. While all hydrangeas are pretty, whether white, or different shades of pink, this cornflower blue shade is beyond beautiful.

In the early spring of 1997 the postal service issued a series of flower stamps, one of Nikko blue hydrangea. One day, several months before Alexandra's wedding, I asked her what I could do for her. She said she wanted me to buy her the flower series of stamps because she wanted to use the hydrangea stamp for her wedding invitations. The wedding invitations were bright white paper stock with cornflower blue engraving. Alexandra knows I'm an avid collector of pretty stamps. The flower series is my favorite. This set included crocus, winter aconite, snowdrop, aster, chrysanthemum and dahlia. They are attractive and I use them all, but none could bring me greater joy than the blue hydrangea stamp.

Brooke's wedding flowers were Nikko blue and white hydrangea in vases on the altar of an old stone church in Stonington Village, as well as the table centerpieces at the reception dinner. A post-wedding celebration the next day in New York City featured huge vases of blue hydrangea.

Often I'm able to buy a pot inexpensively in a grocery store's flower section. I prayerfully water them and see that they get light and fresh air. When we go away, I put them in the refrigerator so that they're there to greet me upon returning. If I'm going to our cottage in Connecticut from our New York apartment, I bring them with me if we don't have too many bags. I put them in an orange rubber tote bag for carrying back and forth. I put a few inches of water right in the bottom of the waterproof tote. When I don't use the orange tote, I cut a plastic water bottle in half and put cut flowers in the bottom half.

Several years ago I was able to keep one plant alive for over three months. The combination of the refrigerator and my bringing it with me was magical. My devotion must have been mysteriously felt.

Recently, I went to my writing room and found my once lovely and healthy plant was completely shriveled up; it was dying in the bright sunlight and had absorbed all the water in its pot. I often say that if you love a plant or flowers, you have to water them. I felt bad. I immediately cut off the stems that looked hopelessly dead and kept the new blossoms intact in the soil. After feeding the plant some water and plant food, and banging the bottom of the stems above the root with a hammer to be sure the water would absorb quickly, I put the pot in the sun. I then put the dried-up stems upside down in ice water for an hour. Sure enough, after they had spent several hours sitting in the sun in a small blue-tinted pitcher, I looked up and both the ones planted in the pot and the ones I'd cut and put in ice water had revived.

What is *it* for you? If you don't have something to be crazy about, find something. What is your irrational passion? What is your shameless joy? List some of your obsessive passions. Some that immediately come to my mind are:

❋ Clear turquoise ocean water
❋ Palm trees
❋ Crab salad for two

✳ Orange and jasmine tea

✳ Sunday afternoon reading a good book
   by the fire with feet up on an ottoman

✳ Daffodils and hyacinths in January

✳ Trudging out into the first winter snowstorm

✳ A ripe avocado with olive oil

✳ Impressionist paintings

✳ Sleeping late

✳ Visiting Venice with my love

✳ Playing with my grandchildren

✳ Eating with chopsticks

✳ Arriving home

✳ Clearing clutter

✳ Sitting together on the porch watching the sunset

✳ Black truffles

✳ The color chartreuse

✳ Paintings by the French artist Roger Mühl

✳ Candlelight

✳ Garden-fresh colors

✳ Chocolate

Of all these irrational passions that I have and you may have, the one that strikes me the most right now is being able to think and write and feel a sense of connection with you through this process. It makes me so happy to express myself about what I love and what I find most beautiful.

✳

BEAUTY IS SERENE AND AT THE SAME TIME EXHILARATING; IT INCREASES ONE'S SENSE OF BEING ALIVE. BEAUTY GIVES US NOT ONLY A FEELING OF WONDER, IT IMPARTS TO US AT THE SAME MOMENT A TIMELESSNESS, A REPOSE—WHICH IS WHY WE SPEAK OF BEAUTY AS BEING ETERNAL.

ROLLO MAY

42

All of Us Love Good News

JOY DELIGHTS IN JOY.

SHAKESPEARE

W e all want some uplift. We want a shot of positive energy. We seem to be starved for pure good news. When people tell me they have good news and bad news I tell them I am delighted to hear good news and I would like a raincheck for the bad news. Sometimes I just feel it is important not to take in bad news if we are not emotionally prepared for it. Often bad news can wait until it can be conveyed appropriately.

I was a columnist for a magazine for six years; I wrote about living beautifully. My message was always encouraging—offering tips, strategies and secrets to help the reader to become happier and live with more beauty every day. The head of marketing took me to a snappy new restaurant in New York and told me she wanted to get me more media coverage, but that good news is hard to sell. If I had a drug habit or was an alcoholic or had been abused as a child, the press would be interested in my having to overcome an addiction or a rotten childhood. I enjoyed a delicious lunch, savoring grilled salmon with organic tomato salsa, and said, "I'm sorry that good news doesn't sell."

While we all love good news, there is a morbid fascination among many people to absorb as much bad news as they can see on television, in the newspaper and in magazines. Horrifying news does sell.

I bumped up against this when I was studying worldwide happiness: Who is happy and why? What do happy people think, feel and do every day? It seemed to me that for every four hundred articles on unhappiness, depression and misery, there was only one article on happiness. When we're aware of all the good in our lives, we can rejoice in good news and enjoy sharing it with others.

My editor and friend, Toni Sciarra, has cultivated the habit of separating good news from not-so-good news when communicating with her authors. Every time one of my books goes back to press, Toni sends me a handwritten note, usually beginning, "More good news . . ."

We can accept inevitable and even tragic occurrences with greater perspective and a higher consciousness when we keep our heart and mind pointed toward all that is good right here, right now. When our energy is founded on goodness, it is natural to want to share it and spread it in all directions. The forces that created this magnificent planet need us to make a joyful noise in appreciation of its continuous beauty, wonders and mysteries. The poet Emily Dickinson's father rang a church bell in Amherst, Massachusetts, at sunset to remind the townspeople to celebrate the awesome colors of the sky.

All good news adds to our sense of well-being and joy. We can never have enough. It doesn't have to be a wedding or college graduation or a trip to Bermuda. We can rejoice in a glorious sunny, crisp fall day. We can have good news when we get an appointment to have our hair cut or to have our teeth cleaned. Peter and I always tell each other we have good news. It could be as simple as announcing that I remembered to buy limes or that Peter found a wonderful article in the newspaper that he wants to read or that the pictures we had developed came out well.

"I have good news." "What?" "I love good news." Be a bearer of good news as often as possible. If your bad news doesn't have anything at all to do with someone you're communicating with, try to keep focused on all that is good in your life right now.

Live a good life. Look for goodness inside your soul and everywhere and communicate it. Ring a bell for no good reason. Life is good.

❋

WHEN SOMEONE DOES SOMETHING GOOD, APPLAUD!
YOU'LL MAKE TWO PEOPLE HAPPY.

SAMUEL GOLDWYN

43

"Yes," "No," and "Wow"

IN THINGS PERTAINING TO ENTHUSIASM, NO MAN IS SANE WHO
DOES NOT KNOW HOW TO BE INSANE ON PROPER OCCASIONS.

HENRY WARD BEECHER

Someone very wise, but I don't know who, said that there need to be only three words in the English language: "yes," "no," and "wow." How do you get from yes to no when necessary? How do you move to yes from no when appropriate? How do you awaken to wow?

Far too many people settle for mediocrity. If we can't make a masterpiece of our own life, whose life can we improve? Wow is our enthusiasm, our awe, our astonishment at all our substance, our potential, our ability to become more loving, kinder, more highly spiritually evolved. "Wow!"

We are thinking animals. We contemplate, wonder and have great curiosity. We will never be complacent. There is too much to explore, to see, to do. Even in a crisis, when it looks as though the dazzling light has been snuffed out, there are surprises that can comfort us.

Years ago Peter and I were returning from an island vacation. The telephone was ringing as we turned the key of the front door. This was not good news. Peter's son had been hit by a fast-moving car and was in a coma. Our fear was too painful for words. We put on coats and went to the airport to get the next flight to Milan. The airline had two seats available—in first class. We sat in seats A1 and A2. After takeoff we were served dinner. Champagne and caviar were placed before us. We toasted each other and sipped; we ate the caviar. When you're going through a serious rough patch, eat the caviar. You'll need it for the journey. It's not an indulgence to treat yourself well under all circumstances. Peter's son fully recovered after months of intensive care and love.

At the reception following the funeral of a dear friend's husband, I whispered, "Dinner at eight?" With a huge smile and a small tear, she said, "Yes, I'll be there."

❈

IS IT NOT BETTER TO INTIMATE OUR ASTONISHMENT AS WE PASS
THROUGH THIS WORLD IF IT BE ONLY FOR A MOMENT?
I HAVE ENJOYED A PERFECT EXHILARATION.

EMERSON

44

Don't Try to Finish Everything Before You Start Celebrating Life

THE LOVE OF PLEASURE IS ONE OF
THE GREAT ELEMENTARY INSTINCTS OF HUMAN NATURE.

ARISTOTLE

There's no time in your life when you'll ever finish everything. We're always in the thick of living. As we enthusiastically embrace a new day, our energy increases, providing us with fresh opportunities to increase our potential. We'll never have enough time to read all the great books we want to read, express all the feelings we have, or complete every project. Life is one big unfinished masterpiece. We'll always be up and running, doing, starting and expanding our world.

An artist has to paint, not have painted. A writer has to write, not have written. Our most important achievements are the ones we haven't started. The best projects are never finished. Life is not a race to be won but time to be cherished. What we can do when we're not working on our chosen projects is to deliberately celebrate life—that is our most serious business at hand.

It's important sometimes to walk away from what we're trying to accomplish in order to embrace a broader perspective. I find that when I play first, everything I do flows more smoothly because I'm receptive to the powerful spirit within. We aren't renewed automatically. We celebrate in order to renew. We celebrate in order to be restored. We practice in order to become better at everything. If you don't use your car, your battery will go dead. If you're not in the habit of dancing regularly, you'll be self-conscious when you dance at a wedding. Celebrating should be a daily habit, not saved up for special events.

We get in the habit of celebrating while we're in the throes of living. Those among us who don't give ourselves the freedom to have pleasure in the active process of each hour are the ones who complain the most about not having enough time—the quintessential excuse for not getting things done and not enjoying your life.

It's nice to have the luxury of time to meditate for an hour before going to yoga class, but we all don't have the luxury of time. We can learn to meditate while walking and carry the lessons of the yoga practice to our desks, our movements and our lives when we're not in class. The physical and spiritual aspects of yoga can be present with us through our mental concentration.

Celebrate with determination, believing that being festive and rejoicing is a central part of a good and productive life. We can honor our time alive by celebrating regular times as well as the most joyful times. We lift our spirits when we have an honestly joyful experience. With practice you will see for yourself that your tasks and projects will be accomplished with greater clarity and ease because, of course, they too are—or should be—a form of celebration.

What are you going to do today? Celebrate life. No one can do this for you, only you can.

❋

CELEBRATION MEANS THE AFFIRMATION OF THE PRESENT,
WHICH BECOMES FULLY POSSIBLE ONLY BY REMEMBERING THE PAST
AND EXPECTING MORE TO COME IN THE FUTURE.

HENRI J. M. NOUWEN

45

Appreciate Everything Good in Your Life

LOVE OF TRUTH ... KNOWS HOW TO FIND AND VALUE
THE GOOD IN EVERYTHING.

GOETHE

*W*e don't need to have happy news to heighten our appreciation. Looking at the big picture, what are you most appreciative about day to day?

Ask people what they most appreciate in their lives. People open up in wonderful ways when they appreciate what they have rather than complain. When we express our appreciation for our health, our spouse, our children and grandchildren, our home, our neighbors, our friends, our job, or nature, we're not nonchalant.

A close friend wrote me a sweet note telling me that I helped her to treasure her daily life. How deeply touched I am to feel that I have influenced someone I love to cherish her life more because of our friendship.

Tell people that you appreciate them and thank them in words spoken or written. When we recognize the magnitude of great souls, the delicate beauty of objects—our consciousness rises.

I appreciate you.

※

RECOGNIZE AND APPRECIATE IMMEDIATELY THAT SOMETHING WAS
ACCOMPLISHED WELL, THAT SOMEONE YOU LOVE LOVES YOU TOO,
THAT YOUR DAY AND YOUR NIGHT HAVE BEEN BEAUTIFUL.
PUT THESE THOUGHTS IN YOUR MEMORY BANK.

PETER MEGARGEE BROWN

* 46 *

Encourage the Child in You to Thrive

IN EVERY ADULT THERE LURKS A CHILD—AN ETERNAL CHILD, SOMETHING
THAT IS ALWAYS BECOMING, IS NEVER COMPLETED, AND CALLS FOR
UNCEASING CARE, ATTENTION, AND EDUCATION. THAT IS THE PART OF THE
HUMAN PERSONALITY WHICH WANTS TO DEVELOP AND BECOME WHOLE.

CARL JUNG

A terrible thing happened when I grew up—I put down childish things. Worse, I stopped reading children's books and put away my teddy bear. The joy reemerged when I gave birth to Alexandra and then to Brooke and I could read wonderful, zany, funny, silly books to them. Then it happened again. They grew up and I stopped reading children's books. Oh, but how glorious it is to have grandchildren to read to and play with, make castles in the sand box with, make "sugar" cookies from sand.

I now am childlike, not childish. I've grown up but not old. When we're able to invent, imagine, daydream and invite invisible friends into our lives, we feel so excited about every possible kind of adventure. We're free, at any age, to create our own fun.

Picasso once said, "It took me a lifetime to learn how to paint like a child." When we are young, we are full of wonder and we are becoming, growing, learning. We get taller, we learn to walk, to talk, to read, to write, to remember, to think abstract thoughts. We are always moving on, excelling, being challenged, being taught, being students of life, of truth, of wisdom.

When we ponder the mysterious power of the beauty of creation, we look at an ocean and feel a part of every wave. When we keep the child in us alive, play is *serious*. We concentrate, and in this trance state, we are outside of our selves, outside of time and inside the spaciousness of the entire universe.

Aim to stay in a state of wonder. This type of superb contemplation arouses awe, astonishment and surprise. Be hungry and thirsty to learn more, to be amazed, to question and explore. When we're filled with curiosity and admiration, we transcend the ordinary. Everything suddenly becomes extraordinary. We gaze with wonder at the marvelous beauty of birds in flight. How do they know where they're going? When we see a rainbow, we see a spectacular ribbon of color. When we gaze at the miracle of a newborn child, we're emotionally aroused, astonished and inspired.

We feel joyous when we focus our concentration, take our time to absorb the surprise of a secret garden or a brilliant pink sunrise, or a star-filled evening sky.

Wonder is wonderful. Keep being wonderfully alive. Think of Claude Monet, who kept his childhood vigor, getting up at three o'clock in the morning to go outside to watch the light arrive in order to paint.

Chase after your dreams. A friend gave me Dr. Seuss's book *Oh, The Places You'll Go!* inscribed, "In celebration of your wedding anniversary and all the love you spread to all the places you go." This *wonderful* book begins: "Congratulations! Today is your day. You're off to great places! You're off and away!" And it ends: "your mountain is waiting. So . . . get on your way!"

We thrive when we have an insatiable appetite for life, when we're eager to get up and get going, and when we're "wonder-ful," full of wonder. We gaze with wonder at the universal forces that miraculously work. I will never stop wondering about what gravity is, what electricity is, how airplanes fly, or the phenomenon of medical science. I absorb the power of the mysterious every day. I want to appreciate all the richness of the universe. The world is full of wonders, inspiring us to learn, to grow, to unfold, to actualize our potential, and uplift our lives and those of others.

WONDER IMPLIES THE DESIRE TO LEARN; THE WONDERFUL
IS THEREFORE THE DESIRABLE.

ARISTOTLE

47

Live Your Autobiography

THE ATTAINMENT OF WHOLENESS REQUIRES ONE TO STAKE ONE'S WHOLE
BEING. NOTHING LESS WILL DO; THERE CAN BE NO EASIER CONDITIONS,
NO SUBSTITUTES, NO COMPROMISES.

CARL JUNG

*I*f you were to write your autobiography, what would you say? We will never fully know ourselves, but no one else could possibly know the whole truth about us, either. No one else understands our hearts, our minds, our souls and our spirits better than we.

What are your beliefs? What are your passions? What are some of the areas of your life that are of great significance to you? Are you living your authentic autobiography? Are you thinking thoughts that increase your sense of pleasure? Do you feel you are living as well as you can?

We are the authors of our own story. There are signs that come to us early on in our journey. We're fortunate when we have the courage to follow our own path, even if there are no road maps and we're not sure of the direction our journey will take.

We are living our life's story in every gesture, with each insight, in all our experiences, in the tough choices we have the guts to make. The only life worth living is the one we take responsibility for choosing. None of us is a hopeless victim being robbed of a joyful life. We can forge a great life only when we're willing to follow our own path toward more light, more happiness, more meaning and more beauty.

To live authentically, to be worthy of trust, to be genuine and true to ourselves, is the greatest way to experience life. When we are authentic, we are the authors (from the Greek *authentikos*) of our life. We are literally living our autobiography.

How resourceful are we in tragic times? How well do we hold up when we confront an illness? How brave are we when we have a financial setback? How well do we meet disappointment? How quick are we to seize an opportunity to enrich our lives? How often do you feel rapture? There are great psychological advantages to wanting to live an exciting adventure, always bringing out the best that's in us.

How you live, where you live, how you spend your time, how intelligent you are mentally and emotionally, is the reality of who you are. The way you dress, where and how you travel, what you like to do for exercise or recreation, are telling your story through your actions, not just your words.

We are the captains; we guide ourselves through this exciting, challenging adventure. If we feel our life's tale is a positive one, one we take pride in, that's good. We can applaud. If we've missed opportunities, not reaching out to enlarge ourselves, our story is sad because we have wasted time and opportunity.

When it rains, fill your well. There will be times when the well is nearly dry. When these times come—and they do in every life—rely on your inner resources. You have them.

We choose how enthusiastically we live our time alive. Our excitement about all aspects of our life is our true and poignant story.

❊

INSIST ON YOURSELF; NEVER IMITATE.
YOUR OWN GIFT YOU CAN PRESENT EVERY MOMENT WITH
THE CUMULATIVE FORCE OF A WHOLE LIFE'S CULTIVATION.

EMERSON

CHAPTER FIVE

Caring

48

You Come First

THERE IS JUST ONE LIFE FOR EACH OF US: OUR OWN.

EURIPIDES

I wish more people would take time to take good care of themselves. When they neglect their their own well-being, we are all drawn into it. Our goal should be to take such good care of ourselves that we're happy, healthy, and productive, sharing our joy of living with others. When we're well, we're resourceful. When we don't take care of ourselves, we're needy. Self-care is in our own hands.

There is a tendency among many decent people to put themselves last. Mothers have difficulty making time for themselves, especially when their children are young. What can happen is that the caregiver may end up with physical and psychological problems. Mothers and nurses have a high rate of burnout. Continual caregiving can be burdensome and depleting if there is no personal renewal.

Whatever responsibilities you take on, put yourself first. Many people rely on you, but this is not the reason you are obliged to care for your own well-being. You should honor yourself and treat yourself with the same esteem you give to others because you deserve to be treated as well as you treat others.

No one gives us time to take care of ourselves. We must take time, make time, and claim time for ourselves every day.

How much stress are you under? Are you stretched too thin? Do you feel overwhelmed by circumstances? What are you doing to relax? If you feel irritable or discouraged, chances are you need to consider the choices you have to remedy the situation. Whatever conditions are going on externally, how you internalize them and how you respond emotionally should be what you examine.

We can't give love from an empty heart. We need to regularly meditate, pray, commune with nature, study, exercise, and have free time to be alone to contemplate. Whether you take up yoga, schedule regular massages, or go on a spiritual retreat, only you can take charge.

No matter what the situation, you are not trapped. You can choose to stay whole, be still, and feel well. The key is to set priorities as well as boundaries. In order to feel more abundantly alive and expansive inside, you need space to breathe. Make regular appointments with yourself to increase your private time. For every hour shared with others, reimburse yourself with a free "me" hour. We all need freedom to be alone. We can't give to the exclusion of attending to our intellectual, emotional, and spiritual life.

Be committed to personal growth, listening to what your heart is expressing. Keep your appointments with yourself. Keep blank spaces in your calendar. Just as birds need space to fly, so we need blank spaces. Having no plans gives us a moment's peace. Aristotle and Joseph Campbell both believed the contemplative life to be the best, most satisfying way to find lasting happiness. Our calendar is our system of reckoning and apportioning time. So much of our time is spent in action—appointments, meetings, calls, and car pools. Resist the temptation to equate ceaseless action with productivity. Don't talk on the cell phone while driving home from work. Don't use this time to catch up with a friend. Take this time to catch up with yourself.

When we awaken to our obligation to be responsible for every aspect of our well-being, we will spend our time wisely, every day, giving ourselves time to replenish our spirits, to awaken to life's meaning for us.

❊

ALL THAT CAN BE DONE FOR YOU IS NOTHING TO
WHAT YOU CAN DO FOR YOURSELF.

EMERSON

49

Inspire Others with Your Vision

YOUR VISION WILL BECOME CLEAR ONLY WHEN YOU CAN LOOK INTO YOUR
OWN HEART. WHO LOOKS OUTSIDE, DREAMS; WHO LOOKS INSIDE, AWAKES.
VISIONS ARE LIKE DREAMS, ONLY THEY OCCUR IN THE WAKING STATE.

CARL JUNG

Shortly after 9/11, the poet and author Maya Angelou came to Lincoln Center to give a talk. She walked onto center stage at Avery Fisher Hall and sang—words that inspired us with her vision: "If it looks like the sun isn't going to shine, look for the rainbow. If it looks as though the sun is really not going to shine, *be* the rainbow." She believes that rainbows are people whose lives are bright, shining examples for others.

Alan Watts, the spiritual visionary who died in 1973, wrote, "Every observer sees the rainbow in a different place. Where, then, is the rainbow?" The rainbow is everywhere when we have eyes to see. The memory of once seeing a double rainbow in Denver, Colorado, arching over the mountains in a deep blue sky, was so inspiring that it is etched in my soul forever. The rainbow can be inside you, patiently waiting to shine after a rainstorm.

Know there is always a rainbow waiting to be seen or felt. We can be rainbows to others through our example. We have vision when we see with our heart and soul as well as with our eyes and intellect. Every bit of wisdom we have gained through experience and from being inspired by people of vision can be shared and passed on to help others. Just as other people have been role models to us, so we can contribute to the inspiration of others through our energy.

When we stimulate our minds and emotions, we breathe life into those around us. We become motivated to action with greater energy, higher ideals, and more reverence for life. Our discernment and imagination are contagious.

When we chase the rainbow, we live in the energy of light, color, inspiration and vision. We are exalted, we are the sun, we are inspirited, instilling courage and encouraging others to inhale this divine guidance. When we have vision, there are no limits to our ability to inspire others to love life more abundantly, to be brave and true to our highest ideals, and to spread light in all directions. Where is the rainbow? Wherever you are.

❋

INSPIRATION AND VISION WAS THEN, AND NOW IS, AND I HOPE WILL ALWAYS REMAIN, MY ELEMENT, MY ETERNAL DWELLING PLACE.

WILLIAM BLAKE

50

Nurse, Nurture and Love

*T*hroughout our lives we are called to care. We nurse a sick loved one back to health. We give physical assistance to those in need. I have great respect for educated, trained nurses who care for the sick or disabled in compassionate, loving ways. Nursing is hands-on. Nurturing, however, is something we can do for loved ones even from a distance. We can be together in spirit, helping others to grow and develop their potential. We can inspire, counsel, listen and cheer someone up without even being aware of the gifts we are sharing. We never truly know the lives we have touched and changed.

I'm humbled to think of all the people we're dependent on every day: the person who shovels the walk after a snowstorm, the teacher who calms a frightened child, the coach who gives up his Sunday for an extra practice session, the person who collects the garbage, the mail carrier who delivers the mail, the person who notices that we're carrying packages and holds the door open for us, the teacher who gave you an award for your enthusiasm in art history, the mother who loves you unconditionally, the boss who sings your praises to the client, the man who delivers your groceries, your spouse who brings you coffee, the doctor who makes a life-saving house call, baby-sitters, the man who repairs the roof, police officers and firefighters, all the people who produce the nourishing foods that keep us healthy and alive, the person who paints the house, the artist who paints scenes you love, the local chef who cooks favorite dishes, the tailor who alters your clothes, the person who cuts your hair, the expert who helps you plan your wedding, writers who inspire you. Emerson believed we should make ourselves necessary for the well-being of others, something we can cultivate and maintain in all our acts of kindness.

We benefit from every good act. Each of us wants to be loved and cherished. The person who believes independence is an ultimate goal may lead a lonely, isolated existence. No man is an island, nor can he live without the help and support of countless people—seen as well as unknown. When we understand that all of life is interdependent, we live with a greater awareness of our appreciation of others. We're able to make more intimate connections, one to another, in this healthy interdependency—parent and child, husband and wife, boss and employee, teacher and student.

My friend Carol took her father in to live with her after he suffered a fall, as she wasn't confident he was yet able to manage on his own after he left the hospital. But nurturing turned out to be a two-way street: during the two months he lived with her family he cooked, grocery shopped and was great company to her children and her dog. Everyone took care of each other, according to their strengths.

Make yourself useful to others. Nourish the opportunity to help someone, to ease their burdens, to give them hope.

❋

KIND PEOPLE HELP EACH OTHER WITHOUT NOTICING
THAT THEY ARE DOING SO.

CHINESE PROVERB

51

Write the Note Now!

*M*y passion for handwritten notes dates back to my early childhood. Handwritten notes, postcards, or letters should be love notes. I don't have the time to be with all of the people I love as often as I'd like, but I can be with them in spirit no matter how near or far apart we are. I understand that a quick note, an affirmation, sending my loving energy to them, can be powerful.

As I said in my little book *Gift of a Letter*, a handwritten letter or note is a gift you give yourself. You are filled with joy as you express your feelings, thanks and affection. Love notes are always appropriate. I've been writing letters and notes from my heart to people of all ages and walks of life for a very long time and I've never once had a letter or note I've sent be misunderstood. Many of the notes I write are to men. I feel confident they take these notes in the spirit they were intended. I want to remind the people I love how much I appreciate them. I have nothing to hide and only love to share.

In your time alive, don't miss the opportunity to fire off a quick note to someone. You never know how meaningful and well timed it may be. We all need to be reminded that we are making a difference to others. You'll never know the tremendous power of your handwritten note. We show our support, understanding and love through our notes, encouraging others to persevere in their rough patches. A handwritten note is special: we open an envelope addressed to us and read words literally written by someone's hand. Email—no matter how convenient—is often less emotionally resonant, mixed up with business requests and information.

I treasure every card and note from my daughters. Length is unimportant. I can put some on my desk and read them over and over. I'm often moved to tears by the generosity of spirit, the affection and deep love that can be conveyed in four or five sentences.

Enjoy the indulgence of having pretty note cards, postcards and stamps. I keep stamped envelopes and postcards in my tote bag, as well as in my purse. Whether I'm at an airport, a train station, or in a taxi, I can whip out a card and dash a note off to a loved one in no time. I bring the person close to me wherever I am when I write to them. If I don't finish in one sitting, I can pick it up when I have a free minute.

Contemplate a few notes you'd love to write that you absolutely know will be treasured keepsakes to the recipients: a teacher, a student, a spiritual guide, a mother's helper, a grandchild at college, your doctor, a dear friend, someone in a hospital, a godchild, a niece or nephew, an aunt, someone who is depressed or unhappy, a child at camp, a floral arranger, a physical therapist, a mentor, a newspaper columnist, a favorite author, a grandparent, an actor, a neighbor, a co-worker or employee.

How can we be useful? How can we help those we love? How can we feel touched in the intimacy of self-expression? When we write a card or note to others, we uplift their spirit as well as our own.

❋

WRITING IS THE ONLY THING THAT, WHEN I DO IT,
I DON'T FEEL I SHOULD BE DOING SOMETHING ELSE.

GLORIA STEINEM

52

Honor Nature

I AM VERY HAPPY, VERY ENCHANTED ... FOR I AM SURROUNDED HERE BY
EVERYTHING I LOVE ... MY DESIRE WOULD BE TO STAY JUST LIKE THIS FOR
EVER, IN A QUIET CORNER OF NATURE.

CLAUDE MONET

*N*ature is a great gift we've been given in our time alive. There are end-less opportunities to explore its beauty and mystery. One of the most significant ways we can rejuvenate ourselves is to surround ourselves in the miracle of nature's beauty.

I worship nature. My reverence has no bounds. This devotion has re-mained and increased throughout the entire course of my life so far. Nature is sacred. I honor her and bless her bounties throughout each day. I've learned patience and I've enriched my joy when I look into nature or, through visual-ization, I call forth her beauty in contemplation. Whether I look at a single snowflake, a sunrise, dew on flowers in the morning, or sunlight sparkling on ocean waves, I feel one with the atmosphere where I am, inspired by the con-tinual gifts I receive by being present.

Nature soothes and relaxes me. Whenever I become tense, I love to run out and embrace the wondrous sights always available to us when we go out of doors. Looking at nature, I have a deeper understanding of my human nature. I learn about beauty, order, variety, mystery, color and change. There's great richness in the inventiveness of nature that always finds solutions to problems. Nothing stays static in nature—the drumbeat of change is in all things.

The flower garden, fruit trees, the beach, grass and mountains inspire me to stay connected to this sacred home where I live. As long as I expose myself to nature's majestic beauty, I am celebrating my time alive every day with joy and often rapture.

I chose to be an interior designer because I wanted to help bring indoors, to the rooms we occupy, the light, energy and refreshing colors we experience when we're out of doors enjoying ourselves in a garden, at the seashore or a lake, in the mountains, or in a forest. Even though Peter and I have flowers, trees, sun and birds in our own tiny walled cottage garden, we also love to take walks because nature's gifts are everywhere, even on the sidewalk.

When I'm in nature, in ideal circumstances, I'm in paradise right here, right now. Do you revere nature? Regularly honor her blessings to us every day.

❋

ARE NOT THE MOUNTAINS, WAVES, AND SKIES,
A PART OF ME AND OF MY SOUL, AS I OF THEM?

LORD BYRON

53

Show Up

ALL SPIRITUAL PATHS HAVE FOUR STEPS: SHOW UP,
PAY ATTENTION, TELL THE TRUTH, AND DON'T BE ATTACHED
TO THE RESULTS.

ANGELES ARIEN

*W*e intuitively want to be in the right place at the right time. Sometimes all we have to do to show our support is to be present. A drama teacher from Chicago tells her students to become a blessing to others throughout the day, adding, "the day is not over yet." Open the door for someone. Help carry someone's groceries to their car or a suitcase to their gate at the airport. Pay a toll for the car behind you or give money to a charity without being solicited. When you make a batch of cookies, give some to a neighbor or the mail carrier.

You never know with any certainty whether there will ever be a better or more poignant time together. You might not hesitate to get on an airplane after your mother's stroke but now when nobody's sick may also be the best time for a family visit. We don't just show up for the sake of family and friends. We do it to keep our appointments with ourselves. In our time alive, we can achieve what is most important if we remain clear about what we most value.

Trying to live with as few regrets as possible makes us sensitive to how fragile and vulnerable all of our lives are. When an occasion is a once-in-a-lifetime event—a major milestone in the life of a child, parent, or friend, a graduation or award ceremony, a wedding or a funeral, we show up because we are drawn to be there, to celebrate, comfort, share love and lend our support. Being in the presence of a loved one during their greatest happy occasions as well as in their most challenging times of loss and discouragement shows compassion.

Life is not lived evenly. There are great exhilarations as well as tragedies that must be endured. When we're willing to live the wide range of experiences openly and with acceptance, we are using our time appropriately. To the best of our ability we pay our respects by showing up.

❀

'LET IT BE OUR HAPPINESS THIS DAY TO ADD TO THE HAPPINESS OF THOSE AROUND US, TO COMFORT SOME SORROW, TO RELIEVE SOME WANT, TO ADD SOME STRENGTH TO OUR NEIGHBOR'S VIRTUE.

WILLIAM ELLERY CHANNING

54

Time Heals

NATURAL FORCES WITHIN US ARE THE TRUE HEALERS OF DISEASE.

HIPPOCRATES

O ur family doctor told us recently that the best-known secret in the medical profession is that time is the best healer. Healing is an active, continuous activity, ever present. We are a part of the cosmos, part of the universe,
that can be regarded as fundamentally ordered. Harmony and order can be and
should naturally be restored to us. There are huge forces at work. The universe is made up of enormous order and consistency interrupted from time to
time by fierce chaos.

The best way to heal and restore your mind, body, heart and soul to health
is to take responsibility for the process. You restore yourself to wholeness.
There is no such person as a healer who can attempt to heal you. Others can
encourage, read your energy, your consciousness, but you and I must heal ourselves. Once we take time to do the inner work needed to regain our physical,
psychological and spiritual wholeness, it is as if we open a window to let in
streams of pure light spreading in all directions. Once we are in this light, we
must make the commitment to ourselves never to turn back.

Take your first step toward radiant well-being. Each one of us must make
this choice. We are health. Choose inner quiet. There can be and often is chaos
all around us, but we can create an atmosphere of inner peace, joy and calm.

You and I have a built-in capacity for wholeness. There is great intelligence
in nature. Sunflowers face the sunrise in the morning and turn their smiling

faces toward the west at sundown. Eric Butterworth, the late Unity spiritual minister, taught that life is always biased on the side of health, wholeness and wellness. We may need medication, but we also need to meditate, to pray, to get in touch with the powerful forces inside us that are healing us. Think of healing as light. The pull of life is upward.

Doctors often advise their patients to go home and rest, to simplify their lives, to re-center themselves. The length of time necessary to heal is always a guess because each situation is unique. When we feel pain, we can view it as a signal that something is wrong. When we're sent home to heal our illness, we can tune out the outer chaos and be of good humor and joy in a familiar environment surrounded by our favorite things and loved ones. We can remember to maintain a healing mindset even to an ailing body.

We need to learn coping skills to be able to soothe ourselves. Each of us learns in a different way to comfort, ease and calm ourselves. Some meditate alone; others walk on a deserted beach. I read inspirational literature and listen to tapes of favorite spiritual guides. The beauty of nature always heals me—a garden, the woods, or the ocean. Whether you want to take a personal day with no agenda, or see a dear friend for a long leisurely lunch, whatever soothes you will heal you. Be aware of the variety of different ways you can care for your whole self and mend your brokenness. Remember, whatever you love to do when you are well will likely be good therapy when you are sick.

Be patient with yourself and others as you take your healing journey. Vow to spend more time in silence every day—both in the morning and in the afternoon. Emerson refers to wise silence. Trust in the divine cosmic wholeness. This is also part of you. Step aside to allow the healing process to take hold and accept your radiant health.

Use all your energy positively. Ease yourself back to being well, whole, and joyous:

Slow down
Calm down
Don't worry
Don't hurry
Trust the process

Spend quiet time alone

Develop your own strategies to reduce stress

Pace yourself

Rest

Laugh at yourself and with others

Give yourself space to breathe

Let go—a greater force is helping you heal

Dwell on love, not loss

Accept wellness, not sickness

Believe that all is well, steering clear of negative thoughts

Affirm your oneness with the universe

Believe that harmony and order are your natural state of consciousness

HEALING COMES FROM GREAT NUTRITION, REGULAR EXERCISE, A HEALTHY
ENVIRONMENT, STRESS REDUCTION, LOVE, POSITIVE ATTITUDE, LAUGHTER,
BREATHING, RELAXING, THE PLEASURE PRINCIPLE, THE HEALING POTENTIAL OF
YOUR MIND AND EVERYTHING ELSE YOU DO *POSITIVE* FOR YOURSELF.

MARCUS LAUX

55

Your Choice: Carefulness or Carelessness?

HAPPINESS IS A CONDITION THAT MUST BE PREPARED FOR, CULTIVATED
AND DEFENDED PRIVATELY BY EACH PERSON.

MIHALY CSIKSZENTMIHALYI

*H*ow well we live our remaining time alive depends, to a large degree, on how careful we are to live with quality in the large and small things we do. To be full of life, to get the best, most productive use from our hours, we should try to be more mindful to try to do our best in every situation.

You always have a choice of how well you manage your personal affairs, your professional life and your relationships with family, friends and community. When you really care, you become more careful because you understand that everything matters. The smallest details make a difference. An inadvertent gesture of insufficient care can cause a disturbance.

Being a careful person is not the same as being a perfectionist. Carefulness is a respectful response to the needs of a situation; perfectionism is an extreme. Winging it, and being too casual, wastes other people's time. If you're proofreading, do it so someone else doesn't have to catch your mistakes. If you're going up or down steep stairs, hold on to the banister. We all know how disappointed we feel when someone wastes our time. Be prepared when giving a speech or a presentation. It's a wonderful feeling to know you've given something your all, especially if it doesn't go off as planned. You know you did everything you could. You don't have to second-guess yourself. You can let go. You can sleep at night. Making it a habit to go the extra mile frees you to take care of yourself. This is the right kind of carefulness. Giving your best is a very liberating cause for celebration.

I prepared for a year when I was invited to give a workshop entitled "Living a Beautiful Life" at the Omega Institute. Most of the talks I give are one hour long; some are up to three hours. I'd never spoken to the same people for sixteen hours over two and a half days. I arrived on campus excited to experience this new format. All the studying helped me to have the confidence to believe this would be a fun and wonderful experience, and it was. The students brought such rich insights to the subject. My preparedness met with theirs, and we all came away feeling exhilarated.

So many people justify being careless by saying that they are relaxed and carefree. But carefree means careless. We have to care about all of our time alive. Being thorough is a virtue. We should assiduously take heed of potential dangers. We need to be especially watchful when caring for a young child.

Choose to run your life smoothly. Try to be thoughtful, not thoughtless, about small, humble tasks. We will continue to drop and break things. We will overlook things we shouldn't have. We will spill coffee on our shirt and get mud on our shoes. But when our lives point toward carefulness, we're minimizing carelessness. Do whatever you need to do now to cultivate careful habits, movements and attitudes. The rewards are in the smooth way your life evolves. Rather than expending frantic energy to rectify snafus, all your energies can be focused on productive and rewarding activities to celebrate fully each moment you have.

❋

IF YOU WANT TO DO A GOOD DEED, DO IT NOW. THE TIME WILL PASS, AND YOU WILL NOT HAVE THE CHANCE AGAIN.

LEO TOLSTOY

Choose Your Friends Wisely

THE GLORY OF FRIENDSHIP IS NOT THE OUTSTRETCHED HAND, NOR THE
KINDLY SMILE, NOR THE JOY OF COMPANIONSHIP. IT IS THE SPIRITUAL
INSPIRATION THAT COMES TO ONE WHEN HE DISCOVERS THAT SOMEONE
ELSE BELIEVES IN HIM, AND IS WILLING TO TRUST HIM.

EMERSON

We know, trust and love our friends. How do these wonderful people come into our lives? How do we meet? His Holiness the Dalai Lama believes, "One of the deepest human desires is to be known and understood." There is nothing more important than someone we love who believes in us and trusts us. When we have this, we have unconditional love. When friends have confidence in our divine potential, it gives deep meaning and significance to our lives.

Even though I suggest we choose our friends wisely, I accept the mystery of how friendships take root and blossom. Each friend is a discrete flower in our garden. Each is different in color, shape and fragrance, but they are all loved. Each of my friends brings out things in me only he or she can. I feel a great sense of joy when I think how richly my friends bless my life each day.

Some of the friends I love most dearly I rarely see because of distance and circumstances. Others I love have left this planet and are on their eternal journey in the light. They are as close to me as though we were together. I love to be able to love a friend completely and, though we haven't been together for ages, we're able to pick right up where we left off, with no sense of separation or loss. I carry my friends with me wherever I am. I'd love to think that my friends think of me often as well and feel uplifted by their thoughts.

Whenever I am with friends we celebrate each other, and are eager to catch up, to learn about all the rich experiences we're having. Friends are gifts from the gods, angels who love us understand us and believe in our goodness and our great potential. Friend to friend, we're here for each other, wishing only for each other's happiness.

While we all wish we could say anything to friends, I don't believe we can. I try to be sensitive about religion, politics and other topics that could potentially divide us. But true friends are never jealous or envious. They are supportive, not possessive. There is no tit-for-tat or keeping score.

Love your friends. Give them dignity and richness, and help make their time alive abundant.

❊

THE MOST WONDERFUL OF ALL THINGS IN LIFE, I BELIEVE, IS THE DISCOVERY
OF ANOTHER HUMAN BEING WITH WHOM ONE'S RELATIONSHIP HAS A FLOWING
DEPTH, BEAUTY, AND JOY AS THE YEARS INCREASE. THIS INNER PROGRESSIVE-
NESS OF LOVE BETWEEN TWO HUMAN BEINGS IS A MOST MARVELOUS THING.
IT CANNOT BE FOUND BY LOOKING FOR IT OR BY PASSIONATELY WISHING
FOR IT. IT IS A SORT OF DIVINE ACCIDENT.

HUGH WALPOLE

57

Actions Can Be Meditations

*W*hat are some of the things you do that you consider to be meditations? I've been meditating for so long that I don't remember the precise year that I began. I don't sit on a mat. Often I don't sit at all. I've taught myself how to make my actions meditations.

I've been contemplative since I was young; I've always found great enrichment from being alone. Once in Japan, I visited Kyoto, where I experienced Zen gardens of raked sand and stones, of "rhythmic nothingness." I became fascinated by the big idea that we plant in the mind whatever we choose to focus on. I now enjoy doing a single object meditation—concentrating on a favorite object, and I also enjoy having the activities that I naturally do in the course of a day turn into meditations. When I iron, my mind empties of everything except the object I'm ironing. I synchronize my inhaling and exhaling with the iron, moving from left to right. I squirt verbena, lavender or rose-scented "linen water" from a plastic bottle purchased at L'Occitane. I spray some starch on a pair of slacks, a tablecloth or a white curtain. I feel completely at peace, at one with the world, and in this reflective absorption in the present moment, I feel enlightened.

I keep a 4 x 6 spiral pad and a pencil (my usual fountain pen and the iron don't work together) near the ironing board because the empty mind becomes full. Now that Peter and I live alone we experience far fewer interruptions than we did when our children were under our wings. But meditation is useful for all of us, whether our homes are fast paced and noisy or calm and quiet. Meditation is focus, and its enemy is rushing. Even if you have never meditated, you can begin where you are right now. We can meditate through our daily activities, by reminding ourselves to slow down, stay mindful of the moment and stay peaceful in the process. Doing the dishes, walking the dog, cleaning the playroom—anything can become more enjoyable when we find a way to focus and meditate.

There are wonderful books written on meditation. If you have never tried to meditate, I highly recommend a book by Jon Kabat-Zinn, *Wherever You Go, There You Are*, or *Peace Is Every Step* by Thich Nhat Hanh.

In meditation, we learn to center ourselves on the precise moment we are experiencing. Through training, we teach ourselves to be so present to the moment that we become one with the action. When you are washing dishes, focus on nothing other than the dishes. There might be numerous times when you forget to focus and you lose your concentration, slipping into your frantic, hurry-rush mode, racing through one action only to start another. But in time, and with powerful determination, you can reprogram your mind by getting into the habit of doing one thing at a time, doing it mindfully and tenderly, and making what you have to do, what you're doing, a devotional exercise.

Claim one day off from the frantic rat race of schedules and continuous chores, and focus on meditation, concentration and relaxation. Before you answer the telephone, think a loving thought toward the person on the other end. Greet the caller with a cheerful communication. When you prune the roses, this can be a meditation. When taking a bath, setting a table, changing bed linens, sipping tea, holding a baby, be conscious of your presence, how you are being completely yourself.

When you turn your necessary actions into meditations, you create clarity and gain wisdom; you are awake and fully aware. In this thoughtful disposition, you feel great inner peace. You are relaxed. Be kind to yourself.

A landscape gardener had a life-transforming experience five years ago at, of all places, a McDonald's. He bolted from his truck, ran to stand in line for a Big Mac and soda, raced back to his truck and fumbled around for his keys.

For twenty minutes he patted his pockets and retraced his steps. He tore the truck apart in search of his missing keys. The keys had vanished! He sat in the driver's seat, rested his head on the steering wheel, and wept. Frank told me recently that this was the universe coming to save him. He believes he would be dead now if he hadn't calmed down. He was so busy building his business, running from here to there, stretched so thin, that his nerves were raw. At a staff meeting one morning, the phone rang and he dreaded the caller: "Oh God, who is calling to complain now?"

He began to meditate. He has now created a meditation garden in his backyard with benches, candles, chimes and a disappearing waterfall. He has a music system that allows him to listen to nature sounds of water and waves, and he also can play his guided meditation tapes. He leaves work now at four in the afternoon, instead of eight in the evening. He goes into his sacred space and meditates, listens, reads, and feels he now has everything he will ever want. This realization has changed everything for Frank. "Now," he told me with a huge smile, "I'm beginning to smell the roses again."

No matter what stage you are in on your life's exciting journey, this is your time. It is essential that you feel that the process is not overwhelming. What meditation teaches me is never to be rough or tough. When actions are meditations, we see beyond what is visible into the expansiveness of our soul's universal essence. Incorporating meditation practices into your everyday activities helps you to center yourself and to enjoy life.

❀

THERE IS A SORT OF GRATIFICATION IN DOING GOOD WHICH
MAKES US REJOICE IN OURSELVES.

MONTAIGNE

58

Cope with the Unexpected

ACCEPTANCE OF WHAT HAS HAPPENED IS THE FIRST STEP TO
OVERCOMING THE CONSEQUENCES OF ANY MISFORTUNE.

WILLIAM JAMES

*W*hen we manage to live in the present moment, we become acutely aware of the precious gift of the miracle of life. Often people wish for everything to stay the same, but that is a still life, not real life.

We have our children's portraits taken; we have pictures and treasured objects to remind us of the chapters of our lives. But life is for growth, for unfolding, for ever expanding our horizons, for actualizing fully our divine potential. Life is change.

Any sense of absolute certainty is an illusion. Wishing for permanence causes suffering. Our time alive comes to an end; this is the only certainty. When, however, we become one with each magical moment we're alive, we carry the love of others who have spent their time before us, as our loved ones will when our time is up.

Prepare yourself, breath by breath, for life's rhythmic transformations as well as for sudden unexpected happenings. Things will always change, and we don't know exactly what will happen next. We thrust ourselves completely into the unknown every day. No one gains foreknowledge of the reality of our lives because we never live backward; we live from moment to moment forward.

We're not in control or able to control events. We prepare for everything we can imagine, but we have to be aware and accept what happens and use it to teach us for the future. The first summer Peter and I were married we rented a house in Nantucket. We invited the icon interior designer Billy Baldwin for dinner. When it came time to light the broiler to grill the swordfish, we discovered we were out of gas for the grill. We did not let this ruin our happy evening. The vegetable and cheese casserole became a chopped salad. Our cold supper was delightful, even though a bit of a surprise.

While we were in North Carolina on lecture tour, Peter fell and injured his knee. He required emergency surgery in New York the next day. I had to postpone lectures in Oklahoma City, San Francisco and Seattle, plus a fun four-day vacation as a birthday gift from Peter in Napa Valley. By accepting the unexpected and unwanted, I was able to manage and go with the flow. Most people are usually understanding when something comes up that is not within our personal control.

When a huge snowstorm was headed toward southeastern Connecticut, Peter and I went to our cottage in Stonington Village to discover the pipes had frozen in the kitchen and the buttery was so freezing cold that all the bottled and canned soft drinks we stored there had exploded, creating quite a mess. What a good thing we went to check on the cottage! We were snowed in for days and had an unexpected winter vacation!

To live, we must prepare ourselves for change—not always what we want or what we expect, just what is. Robert Frost's wise advice, "the best way out is always through," helps us to identify reality, to understand the uncertainties, and to cope as best we can.

How strong are you when you have to face unexpected situations, when all your plans have to be put on hold or are canceled? How brave are you when you are faced with a crisis? I've discovered that I am at my best, that I rise to the occasion, when I'm in a serious situation. Having been through many family crises, I've learned with each one how to accept what is. We never know the extent of our inner resources until we are challenged.

Our priorities can change in an instant. When we learn of a relative or friend being in an accident, we drop everything. Everyone understands when we have a crisis in our life. We always do what we have to do because there is no other time or way.

Not all of the unexpected is bad news, but because of life's realities some certainly is. Rather than illness or death, maybe you discover that you're preg-nant—surprise! You are completely unprepared. You thought you were sure there was no way you could become pregnant. But you are the statistic. In time, after the shock, you realize that this child is the best miracle of all, and you can't imagine your life without your surprise son.

As you move forward, remain open to what comes to you. There will be many gifts that rise from the ashes. Prepare now for whatever happens by spending time enriching your inner life so you won't be thrown around in a storm. And remember that in the eye of a storm, there is a calm center—that is you. You are not alone. We all experience unexpected, sometimes shocking, realities. We learn to cope well because, even in these circumstances, we can draw on our inner resources and our faith, rising to meet the challenge with courage and love.

·   ❋

NOTHING IN THIS WORLD CAN ONE IMAGINE BEFOREHAND,
NOT THE LEAST THING. EVERYTHING IS MADE UP OF SO MANY
UNIQUE PARTICULARS THAT CANNOT BE FORESEEN.

RAINER MARIA RILKE

59

This Too Will Pass

*L*ife is a journey, certainly not a destination. Whatever you are experiencing now—whether you are in a heightened state of joy, expressing your creativity, being useful and fully alive, or whether you are going through a rough patch, this is where you are right now. Your baby becomes a toddler, and then goes off to preschool, school, college and then career, marriage and children to follow. You mother dies just before your wedding and will never experience her grandchildren. As painful as some situations are, they are often bittersweet. You were able to love your mother for the twenty-nine years you shared. Your wedding day is once in a lifetime; you should live this day completely, carrying your mother's spirit with you throughout the joyous festivities.

The brilliant radiance of a joyful family vacation is soon over, the children go back to school and you go back to work. Because nothing under the sun ever lasts—no emotion or experience—we can be reassured that the most excruciatingly painful times transform and transcend into acceptance. We gain greater love and understanding from accepting our pain. In the happiest hours we share, these good times will sustain us when we need to remember that all of our time is volatile.

The great wisdom is not to become too attached to things or to the outcome of an important event. Love each moment for what it is, but don't cling too tightly; nothing is ever all bad or all good. There are beautiful moments in hard times because we remember the sunny days when our spirits were refreshed. I've learned I'm part of something larger than myself. Everything passes, even pain. Everything is in the process of transition. This too shall pass. Nothing lasts forever. Good things don't last, either. The beauty of the sunset or daffodils in a vase are finite.

How well do you bounce back? How do you uplift yourself when you feel discouraged or just plain sad? I wear bright clothes. I surround myself with flowers, listen to favorite classical music, try to get more sleep, have a massage, have my hair done, go for long quiet walks and read Aristotle and Emerson as well as other well-selected poetry. I eat lots of fruit and vegetables. I try to think about all those I love who love me, and I try to live my time alive as well as I can.

From all my times of loss, I've been able to rise to the occasion, to find inner strength in my brokenness. Wordsworth realized that "a deep distress has humanized my soul." There is power in pain just as there is power in love. We feel at the heart of our humanness a shared pain, a universal understanding that we all experience loss of others as well as our own death. I bounce back quickly when I deliberately try to center myself. Because I know it is my responsibility to remain positive, I take whatever steps are necessary to regain my spirit even if it requires some time off from responsibilities. I know I am not alone. There is a mystery in pain that brings an inner peace and joy that no one can take from us.

We proceed, moving past and beyond each experience, always becoming more appreciative for the gift of our life. When we use our time well, we will always be able to stay on our path. Every significant experience has its nobility where there is great care, tenderness and love.

I've come to understand that every single happening in our life becomes part of our character and soul. We are being shaped and transformed by each opportunity to care, to know, and to love ourselves better and to become enlightened along the way.

❀

THE HUMAN SPECIES IS FOREVER IN A STATE OF CHANGE, FOREVER BECOMING.

SIMONE DE BEAUVOIR

CHAPTER SIX

Purpose

60

Write Your Own Purpose Statement

THE HIGHEST PURPOSE OF THE HUMAN SPECIES IS TO
JUSTIFY THE GIFT OF LIFE.

NORMAN COUSINS

*W*e learn so much about the character and nobility of people at their funerals. When someone's time alive is over, others tell stories, share
memories, and reveal a person's integrity, authenticity and decency. I'm a great
believer in a homily and eulogies at services of remembrance in praise and celebration of a well-lived life.

How you choose to live your life is of great significance to you, to me, to
the universe. And when your time alive has come to a close, your obituary may
be in a newspaper. When someone has found his life's purpose, we are amazed
by the rich textures, accomplishments and fullness of a focused life.

In three or four sentences, write your own purpose statement for your life's
direction. When you concentrate on your personal and professional life, what
are your intentions? What purpose do you want to pursue as you find enjoyment in the life you have led?

For some of us, a sense of purpose comes naturally, often early in life. We
begin to wonder and to question where we best fit in, how we can intelligently
use our gifts and pursue our unique path. How can we remain true to ourselves
throughout our entire life? Once we know our aim, our goals, we can put
bright lights on our life. We can stretch ourselves to live with more commitment and more determination that leads us to greater accomplishments.

Chinese wisdom teaches us that every bird alive in the universe always knows where to make her nest. Birds know their purpose in life. We're the wisest among creation, yet we often don't know what our life's purpose is.

What are you ecstatic about? What offers the most sublime meaning? What is the one thing that is necessary for you in your life? What is the best life for you to live? Everything becomes clear to us when we focus our energies on what makes us feel most alive and most useful.

With all the pressures of a fast-paced, result-driven society, how do we become calm and pursue our highest purpose, following it no matter where it will lead?

What have you always wanted to do? Are you following your dream? As soon as we love our vocation, our life has great purpose. Have you discovered your calling? Why are you doing what you're doing? What are you looking for in your time alive?

When you feel your life has purpose, everything seems to fall into place as one big circle. Everything is seamlessly connected; there is no beginning or ending, just one continuous flow of giving of yourself from your open heart. The energy field of the universe comes rushing to help you. You're able to think big and dare boldly because you know from experience how it feels to be exhilarated, to thrive on the challenges of trying to make a difference. To live, to give, and to serve in unique ways that only you have the knowledge and awareness of, directs your course with focus and love. As if miraculously, suddenly you see and understand how everything aligns with your purpose. You're able to see the big in the little. Your love of letter writing as a young child evolved into your passion to be a writer as an adult. You learn about your interests from the books you choose to read, the music you listen to, the courses of study you follow, and you know what you seek to accomplish. Who do you believe your true Self to be? What is keeping you from pursuing your dreams? What engages you? What fills up and lights up your heart? What interests you to the point of bursting?

In order to become a master, you will have to devote your life to seeking the answers to the most unanswerable questions. Rainer Maria Rilke called this "living the question." You find solutions by forging headfirst into the immensity of your life's purpose. Is your purpose to live an inspiring life? To make kindness your religion as His Holiness the Dalai Lama has by the grace of his teachings and example? To be a devoted truth seeker? To be a poet, an artist?

Establish your purpose statement when you are alone. This exercise requires brutal honesty. Your life's purpose defines you. Following this path requires a focused commitment to stay the course and achieve your excellence.

❀

LET US DEFINE A PURPOSE OURSELVES, LET US REGULATE OUR LIVES ACCORDING TO THE PURPOSE WE SET. THEN OUR ACTS, OUR WORDS, AND OUR MOODS WILL ACQUIRE A UNITY AND WILL HARMONIZE WITH THIS PURPOSE. AND WE MUST CONSIDER THIS HARMONIZATION AS OUR DUTY, THAT IS, OUR HAPPINESS.

NIKOS KAZANTZAKIS

61

Act, Don't React

I HAVE GAINED THIS BY PHILOSOPHY: THAT I DO WITHOUT
BEING COMMANDED WHAT OTHERS DO MORE ONLY FROM FEAR OF THE LAW.

ARISTOTLE

Once we follow our purpose, we get things done that we believe to be important. We no longer wait around for someone else to give us assignments or approval. Choose what you want to accomplish. Make your plans. Set short-term goals as well as thinking ahead to where you want to be on your journey five years from now.

We all plunge into the depths of the unknown every time we act. We shape our actions according to our discoveries, the knowledge we gain, the insights we pick from our chosen activities. Our convictions lead us to the right actions. We do what we most believe is important. Our strong belief creates success. We have to have faith in ourselves, and be aware of our feelings. Without waiting for others to approve or disapprove, we must quietly act according to what we know is the best way to conduct ourselves.

Draw a circle. Where in this circle are you located? You are in the center, not at the perimeter. We all want to be free to live according to what we value, what we believe to be a good, well-lived life.

Try not to get stuck in reaction mode, bobbing around from here to there like a cork in the sea. I observe many people in robot reaction mode. When we act on our own accord, we are not reacting to someone else's actions. We can agree to disagree, we can help out where there is a need, but it is our own life we are meant to be living. If we all thought for ourselves and had the confidence to follow through on our own sense of purpose, imagine how well off the world would be.

Live in the center of your circle. This is the center of your gravity. Here you won't feel pulled and tugged in all directions. Focus on your personal growth, commitment and discipline. Don't look around the circle. Look within and act from your heart, from your deepest convictions. Write down what you want to do and begin now. There will never be a better time to act. If someone comes to you with a "big idea," pause. Retreat in silence to consider the proposal. Unless this "big idea" resonates with your life's purpose, it may not be right for you. Every moment you must choose to have your actions be your own.

Every genuine loving gesture and action is a blessing to others. Believe in yourself and joyfully go about your *doing*. Do what you believe is the right thing. Try to be inner-directed rather than outer- or other-directed. Act from your center—not reacting to the chaos and confusion of others.

❋

UNLESS WE HAVE FAITH IN THE PERSISTENCE OF OUR SELF, OUR FEELING OF IDENTITY IS THREATENED AND WE BECOME DEPENDENT ON OTHER PEOPLE WHOSE APPROVAL THEN BECOMES THE BASIS FOR OUR FEELING OF IDENTITY WITH OURSELVES. ONLY THE PERSON WHO HAS FAITH IN HIMSELF IS ABLE TO BE FAITHFUL TO OTHERS.

ERICH FROMM

You Never Know

*M*y spiritual guide, John Bowen Coburn, was a great friend of my aunt Ruth Elizabeth Johns. They went to Union Theological Seminary together. John became an Episcopal minister and bishop; my aunt became an international social worker. The church didn't allow women to become ministers in the 1940s. I met John as a teenager and we became friends when he became the minister of the church I attended in New York City. John married Peter and me at St. James Church in 1974.

When John's wife was in the hospital giving birth to their second child, a son, their daughter Annie mysteriously died of crib death. He wrote a book about Annie—a book about death, a book about love. Why did Annie die in her sleep? One of John's friends had a child who was institutionalized for mental illness. John was speechless when he communicated with his friend. Eventually he inquired, "What do you make of this?" John's friend simply said, "You never know."

We really never know the cause of anything or what will happen next. Understanding this truth helps us to live our moments as intensely, as lovingly, as possible. You never know when you tuck your baby into bed at night if it will be the last time she is alive. You never know if your husband will survive his heart operation. You never know if this present moment is the best you'll ever live in your time alive. We literally never know what will happen next—good or bad. A Silicon Valley scientist, Bill Joy, understands human nature: "It's hard for people to accept that something will happen if it hasn't happened yet."

What we want from life can be in our own hands. We should believe in our own powers. The tragic stories are well known of people who lived superficially until it was too late.

I'm humbled to come face to face with the future that is unknown and not guaranteed. We live our lifetime one breath at a time. Every breath we take provides us with infinite possibilities. Our life is a process marked by gradual changes as well as instantaneous occurrences—a loved one has an automobile accident, your home is destroyed in a hurricane, your dog runs away from home, your grandson becomes seriously ill.

Because we never know, accept all your blessings right here, right now.

✳

TO CHANGE ONE'S LIFE, START IMMEDIATELY, DO IT
FLAMBOYANTLY, NO EXCEPTIONS.

WILLIAM JAMES

63

Practice Active Virtue

THE SIMPLEST, QUICKEST AND SUREST MEANS TO BECOMING KNOWN AS
A VIRTUOUS PERSON IS TO WORK ON YOURSELF, TO ACTUALLY BE VIRTUOUS.
EXAMINE EACH VIRTUE, AND YOU WILL SEE THAT THEY ALL WERE
ACHIEVED WITH WORK AND EXERCISE.

SOCRATES

*M*oral excellence is an achievement. Virtue is acquired through habit, exercise and spending time to improve yourself daily. When someone is commendably good, it is because that person spends time focusing on elevating his inner life.

Our actions should echo the innermost depths of our being. When we are true to ourselves, our souls will manifest their pure light in our outward acts. This is an inward-out process of self-reflection and self-expression. The pleasure comes from the virtuous activity. When we're at our best, with the wind at our back, and the sun shining brightly in our heart, every act of virtue will increase our sense of purpose.

Socrates instructs us to work on ourselves. We cultivate virtue when we both study virtue and practice it in the trenches of our daily activities. It is not enough to read books about being mindful only to close the books and act half-crazed in the chaos of our hectic family life. The place to practice active virtue is in our daily lives. Goodness and love can be experienced in our home, at the workplace, at the gas station, in the grocery store, at the train station or wherever we are.

Make a list of virtues that you recognize as excellent, wise principles to live by. Some of the virtues I try to practice are integrity, self-acceptance, self-understanding, self-forgiveness, attentiveness and perseverance. What are some virtues that you value as wise and supremely good? What are some universally accepted virtues you believe you actively practice daily?

One of my virtues is that I am tenacious; I hold fast to my vision of what I want to achieve. I wrote *Daring to Be Yourself* while lying on my back using a space pen because of a back injury. If I had not agreed to lie down for three months, I would have required surgery.

When I was taken directly from the doctor's office to a nearby hospital for treatment of pneumonia, I used the back of the doctor's patient information sheets to write *Style for Living* because the manuscript was due at the publishers soon and I didn't want to miss my deadline. I try not to make excuses.

Thomas Edison believed that sticking to it is genius. Because teachers thought he was mentally retarded, he was home schooled. Albert Einstein's theories were wrong 99 percent of the time, but he was right one percent and is considered a genius. I'm not considered a genius, but I am a plugger. I value my perseverance. I rarely give up what I believe to be important.

Practicing active virtue takes courage because you have to act on your convictions without giving up. Keep on keeping on because this is what we must all do. The thirteenth-century Persian Sufi poet Rumi believed that "when you do something from your soul, you feel a river moving in you, a joy . . ." Our joy is pure when we believe we are meant to be doing exactly what we are engaged in—actively, emotionally, and spiritually.

When we believe in ourselves, when we are in touch with our feelings, when we have a burning need to make the most of our time, we are actively virtuous. The daily practice of virtue makes us flow like a river toward greater clarity and light.

❋

THE VIRTUE OF A PERSON IS MEASURED NOT BY
HIS OUTSTANDING EFFORTS, BUT BY HIS EVERYDAY BEHAVIOR.

BLAISE PASCAL

64

What Is Your Deepest Desire?

TO WISH IS LITTLE: WE MUST LONG WITH THE UTMOST
EAGERNESS TO GAIN OUR END.

OVID

One of my favorite poets is Ovid, an ancient Roman romantic known for his explorations of love. He believed that what we long for we already have because the power to achieve our desires lies within. We spend our whole lives with inner longings that take possession of us. We are never more alive than during those fluid moments of light, clarity, beauty and love.

We all yearn to have our desires met. While we are alive we should regularly take stock to sense and feel what we really want. Where do you choose to focus your energy? So many people are driven, so busy that there is a blockage in their hearts that restricts the open space. The candle gets snuffed out. The light becomes dark. Even in the darkness, in the busy-ness of overcrowded schedules, too much to do in too little time, in the anxious confusion, in the noise, the chaos of deadlines and pressures, we have moments when we pay attention to our inner longings.

When our hearts get overcrowded, we lose our life force. This energy wants to be joyfully expressed in pure pleasure. While we are alive with a body, with our five senses, now is the time to take as much pleasure as humanly possible. Through sensuous gratification, love of people, animals, nature's awesome beauty, as well as passion for our work, we can celebrate our all-too-brief earthly existence.

We should find as many outlets that are a source of enjoyment and delight as possible. I'm a sensualist through and through. I am highly appreciative of the pleasures of sensation. I have a huge appetite for the physical senses. I'm also a romantic person. I enjoy beautiful atmospheres that open my heart wide. I seek to bring more color, energy and joy to celebrations—birthdays, anniversaries, or just quiet nights at home.

We have our five senses. They are a powerful gift to us to use every moment we are alive. Taste the corn, smell the peonies, hear the Beethoven symphony, touch the sand, see the sunset. I am often moved to tears just by seeing lovers celebrating moments tenderly. Regularly take stock of what your heart desires. What are some of your unedited desires? Treat yourself to quiet times when you give yourself unrestricted freedom to expand yourself into the depths of your being.

Desire to know yourself purely. Desire to be understood. Do you have a deep desire for your inner longings to manifest throughout the rest of your life? I understand that we can't ever be completely fulfilled. We will always be yearning for a sense of oneness with all of creation.

Every moment we are being given clues to our deepest desires. By gently listening, we will hear and know. May your desires be energizing and pure in order to deepen and raise your consciousness of your immense potential for living.

❈

IT IS A GREAT HAPPINESS TO HAVE WHAT YOU DESIRE;
BUT IT IS AN EVEN GREATER HAPPINESS NOT TO WANT MORE
THAN YOU ALREADY HAVE.

MENEDEMUS

65

Value Your Time from One to Ten

ALL MY POSSESSIONS FOR A MOMENT OF TIME.

ELIZABETH I

*I*f you value your time as ten—the highest possible on the scale of one to ten, you are living your time alive wisely. Time awake, aware and free to spend however we feel is the best possible way, is exceedingly valuable—literally priceless.

Time is, of course, a limited commodity. Everyone alive has only so much time. We can take off our watch. We can forget to wind the clock, but time marches forward whether we pay attention or not. I love clocks and I always wear a watch (when I'm above water), because time is ticking as I breathe and I like to be aware of how well I choose to spend it. We are all given life one day at a time. How do you choose to live this day?

Every minute you are alive you are spending your time in some specific way. If you are earning money, what is the cost of the time spent to do so? What amount of time is required to earn money? You gain money but give of your time. You and I need to carefully weigh the exchange. Money is a medium that can be exchanged for goods and services and used as a measure of value in the marketplace. If we have a pot of gold, it has a certain value. But if we have money and have no time, it is worthless.

Time bankruptcy is far worse than financial bankruptcy because, in theory, we can always go out, roll up our sleeves, and with our long right arm, earn more. Western civilization is often uncivilized by mistakenly believing—or at least hoping—that money buys the right to happiness.

Ben Franklin was wrong when he said time is money. Those of us who value the importance of time as a ten know that time is life; money is a material commodity. Used properly, money buys us time. We can hire people to help us maintain our lifestyle, actually saving us time. But, unfortunately, all too often, greed takes over and enough is never enough. One pot of gold is no longer enough. The nineteenth-century Boston parish minister, William Ellery Channing, begins his "symphony" with the wisest words. "To live content with small means . . ."

We have so many keys. We lock up our money and we guard our property with security gates and alarm systems, but the keys we have are never the right ones to open up our lives to pure joy. The best, most useful, key is the one that is the most protective of our time. From one to ten, how important is money to you in your remaining time alive?

Value every hour you spend. You are giving a portion of your life. You can always acquire more money, but time is finite. One of life's great paradoxes is that living "content with small means" increases the value of everything: the stillness, quiet listening, nature's beauty and life's profound mysteries.

Only time can give us the opportunity to deepen our sense of purpose. Time is there for us to study truth, to focus on beauty and love, and, when we're fortunate, "time will tell"—it will lead us to wise ways to give back to the world in gratitude for the amazing grace of being alive.

❋

THEY DEEM ME MAD BECAUSE I WILL NOT SELL MY DAYS FOR GOLD;
AND I DEEM THEM MAD BECAUSE THEY THINK MY DAYS HAVE A PRICE.

KAHLIL GIBRAN

66

Love What You Do;
Do What You Love

*H*ow many people can honestly say that they love what they're doing and doing what they love? It seems reasonable that if we love what we're doing, we'll find joy.

Too many people can't wait to get through situations, wanting them to be over with, so they can go back to their normal routine. Who wants to continuously feel burdened by their life's happenings? When one hurdle is behind us, another one is in front of us. This is the nature of real life.

I'm a believer in finding ways to love what we're doing. If I'm meant to be involved in a situation, I look within my heart and try to find what is precious, find what I love, where there's joy. Remember, this is your life. If you only feel the pain without the pleasure, it's reasonable to assume that life, day to day, wouldn't be a whole lot of fun.

If we can't lighten up and brighten up, laugh at ourselves as we find ourselves in amusing predicaments, see the humorous side of the moment, as well as the serious, we will go through our days with heavy heart and hand.

We often spend time, energy, ideas and money—our four major resources—on things that are not only unimportant, but destructive and joyless. Because we are in charge of what we think, we bring our minds with us in every moment, even into our subconscious hours of sleep. In order to love what we're doing and do what we love, we need to open up our hearts wide. We want intuitively to connect to our vital center, the source of our being.

Our heart is the repository of our deepest and most sincere feelings and beliefs. I live my life from my heart because my direct, pure experience can be joyful when I have the right attitude. Why dread a situation when we can focus on what will be fun?

We shouldn't diminish ourselves because we are in a situation we don't choose. If you are at a family reunion and there are several negative people there, be a good listener. Everyone loves to talk. Ask each person what is most exciting about his or her life right now. Let them talk. You will help bring out the best that's in them. A lot of people in our lives are insecure and are intimidated by us even though they pretend to be superior. When we can remain true to our higher selves when challenged, we will not only ease tension and awkwardness, but we will be raising our consciousness in the trenches of real life.

Most of us have one or more extremely awkward family members. If we're in an uncomfortable situation, we're better able to navigate it by seeking a fun, joyful, positive aspect. Try to make the very best of the time you're in the situation. Enjoy the other people, appreciate the food, spend time with some young people, and remember the five-hour rule I wrote about in *Things I Want My Daughters to Know*: You never have to be with anyone longer than five hours! It goes both ways. Some people really don't choose to be with us. We can give them a break. Love, and our capacity for generosity and compassion, comes from the center of a loving heart.

Our basic disposition and character are matters of our heart. We need only to listen and respond to the intelligence of our heart for guidance. When we live from our center, we remain in the flow. We may be in unloving situations, but we should keep an open heart. I've learned through painful experiences to listen and remain silent. If I react, I will be compromising myself. Try not to say anything in self-defense that is unloving. Silently walk away from people who are uncaring. We can keep our inner light shining brightly in all the circumstances that are beyond our control.

Our purpose on earth is to be fulfilled. Our success in life depends on our continuously finding circumstances that express and fulfill our higher self. If you can't find what you love to do, create situations that bring you joy. If you can't be with your grandchildren, invent ways to be involved with them when you are separated: call them, write them, and send them books, so you feel the love alive in your heart. Have a lunch party for your busy daughter and invite her best friends, who she hasn't seen in several months. We want to be together but our schedules are so full. By having such a luncheon, my daughter and I were able to catch up. I had a great time as one of the girls!

Reach out to live the life that encourages you to do what you love with loved ones. By being outgoing and showing your love to loved ones, you will find great pleasure in the anticipation of your times together. There is joy in the sheer love you feel for others that is reinforced by your action. Our reward for loving what we do is the opportunity to know ourselves better, to grow wiser and feel a deep sense of connectedness to others.

Rainer Maria Rilke wrote of "the winged energy of delight." Loving what you're doing takes the pressure off, lightens the difficult situations, and spreads joy.

✳

FIND A PLACE WHERE THERE IS JOY,
AND THE JOY WILL BURN OUT THE PAIN.

JOSEPH CAMPBELL

67

Choose to Live a Life of Significance

I HAVE ONE LIFE AND ONE CHANCE TO MAKE IT COUNT FOR SOMETHING ...
I'M FREE TO CHOOSE WHAT THAT SOMETHING IS ... MY FAITH *DEMANDS*
THAT I DO WHATEVER I CAN, FOR AS LONG AS I CAN, WITH WHATEVER I
HAVE, TO TRY TO MAKE A DIFFERENCE.

JIMMY CARTER

*B*ecause we live day to day doing ordinary tasks, sometimes we get bogged down in the details and don't always see the significance of our actions. The more we understand the consequences of the ordinary things we do every day, the more vital energy we can invest in them. Everything in our lives has more meaning than we can possibly imagine.

When we come to see that our individual life has great value, we can spend our time in pursuit of excellence in all our choices and actions. Whenever we don't approach life with a sense of reverence, dignifying the most humble task, we lose the clarity of our character. We are important when we want to do whatever we can to make a contribution to the world. We have great capacity. We can wisely use what we've been given to try to make the planet more loving, safer and more peaceful.

Living with significance is a goal that is achieved moment by moment, thought by thought, step by step, as we develop our characters. We should do what only we can do, and be what only we can be, bringing to the world what we are uniquely qualified to provide.

Take time to do everything well. This is an important first step. If you volunteer to do a fundraiser for a favorite charity, be sure you begin your preparations early. Stay focused on not rushing or being anxious. Be ahead of time, not behind. The key is to continue to love the process of what you're doing. It's far better to take on less and feel good about the time you invest in doing the best you can in whatever situation you're in, than to take on too much and feel frustrated by a lack of fulfillment.

When we choose to live a life of significance, we sharpen our value of time. Significance is a worthy goal, involving quality and time management. When we want to do our best and have a strong sense of purpose, the total of our days adds up to many accomplishments we're proud of. Pay attention to your feelings. Do you feel that you are giving back to your community? How have you chosen to give back to the universe?

Everything you think and feel that is significant will generate goodness. The world needs you to contribute all that you have.

✳

CONFIDENCE THAT ONE IS OF VALUE AND SIGNIFICANT
AS A UNIQUE INDIVIDUAL IS ONE OF THE MOST PRECIOUS POSSESSIONS
WHICH ANYONE CAN HAVE.

ANTHONY STORR

68

Balance and Moderation Are Keys to a Purposeful Life

HAPPINESS IS FOUND IN THE GOLDEN MIDDLE OF TWO EXTREMES.

ARISTOTLE

I cannot think of a more decent person, with a stronger sense of social justice, than my Aunt Betty. She always wanted to do the right thing. Of all the wonderful qualities of this remarkable pioneering woman, who felt the world was her front lawn, who had friends in all corners of the globe, my favorite was her sense of moderation.

I remember once having dinner with her at her close friend's home in Rangoon, Burma, in 1960. Dr. Suvi had a spectacular orchid garden and was the lead surgeon at the Rangoon General Hospital. I sensed he was in love with my aunt. After a tour of the hospital and a memorable walk through his garden, we were seated for lunch. My sister, Barbara, my cousin Betty, Aunt Betty, Dr. Suvi and I held hands, squeezed, and began a most memorable banquet full of laughter and tears. Dr. Suvi had lived in Hyderabad, India, for many years and had acquired a taste for extremely spicy curry. We dug in and all of us were on fire! Our noses began to run, our eyes were full of tears. Ice water was not enough to quench the heat. Dr. Suvi put his hands together—*clap, clap*—and ordered beer for all of us from a waiter dressed in white and wearing a red hat. Aunt Betty— a teetotaler—was served first: "Betty, this is for medicinal purposes." As we were served the beer, she told Dr. Suvi we were not allowed to drink alcohol. "Betty, dear, sip your beer and remember, moderation in everything, even virtue." We gulped down ice-cold beer and enjoyed the curry enormously.

On the same world trip I learned the concept of yin and yang, the Chinese dualistic philosophy. Yin is the passive cosmic principle—as in the moon, shade—the female element. Yang is the active cosmic principle—the sun, light—the male element. Everything carries yin and yang. To be whole and healthy, we need to balance our yin and yang energies. When they are not in harmony, we may develop health problems. We need to blend and balance them to bring harmony to our lives.

Feng shui, the Chinese art or practice of positioning objects—graves, buildings and furniture, is based on a belief that patterns of yin and yang and the flow of ch'i (our vital energy) have positive and negative effects. Feng means wind and shui means water.

If something feels right in a space, it is right. If something doesn't feel right, it isn't right, and we can change it. As an interior designer, I constantly strive for a harmonious arrangement of objects that is satisfying to our senses and spirit. People and spaces, as we all know, have an aura. There is an invisible breath of energy that is intangible but distinctive that seems to surround a person or thing. The quality of the atmosphere can be as gentle as a fresh breeze.

How sensitive are you to the atmosphere around you, to the energy of people and places? After you've spent time with someone, how do you feel afterward? Do you feel uplifted and better than before your visit? When you spend time in a room, do you feel the refreshing energy of wind and water? Feng shui helps us to understand that there are always going to be opposing forces and influences in life. Harmony is the result of a subtle balancing of yin and yang energy. This applies to our emotional life, as well as to the decoration and design of a room.

Balance is key to a healthy emotional state. The ancient Roman lyric poet Horace taught us that a balanced mind "I find for myself." We bring everything into our minds and then, through meditation and self-reflection, balance the negative and positive thoughts and emotions. We accept what we cannot change and transcend the darkness. We learn to control our emotions through our mental discipline. This inner work is essential in order to spend our time alive focusing on our purpose.

When we're acutely aware how valuable our time alive is in order to fulfill our sense of purpose, we see how balance and moderation are of vital importance to a good life. The lively personal essays of my favorite French essayist, Michel de Montaigne, are considered the highest expression of sixteenth-century French prose. He believed that "greatness of a soul consists not so much in soaring high and in pressing forward, as in knowing how to adapt and limit oneself."

We all know how delicate the balance is between too little and too much: too little exercise; too much food; too much time in solitude, not enough time with friends; too much traveling and not enough time with the family; too much head work and not enough body work; too many tasks in too little time; too few celebrations; too much time at the office.

Wisdom teaches us that more than enough is too much for our own good. Whenever we strike a healthy balance between not enough and too much, we're aiming at what the ancient Greeks called the Golden Mean. Who could argue that the golden mean between the two extremes is the ideal state of equilibrium? The good and purposeful life requires a continuous effort to be in a state of equilibrium where we are stable mentally and psychologically. There is no possibility for lasting happiness and well-being without emotional stability. When we are on an even keel, we feel happy.

There are times in our lives when even the happiest occasions and celebrations can be so time pressured that the stress creates an imbalance. Unable to relax and enjoy the moment-to-moment experiences, we live in crisis mode. We learn our life lessons the hard way. One of the most important lessons to learn is the art of balance. I traditionally gave a dinner party for all our friends who came to the Roger Mühl art opening every other November. Coincidentally, the date was always close to or on my birthday. One year I was on book tour, flying into New York and flying out again the next day. Rather than sending engraved invitations, I made a few phone calls. I invited friends to come for supper after the opening. We had one of the happiest evenings I can remember. We were eleven people instead of twenty-four. Instead of three separate seating areas, we were all cozy at one extended farm table. We all held hands before eating, feeling an intimate bond being together. The small group created a different kind of energy. Everyone participated in the conversation, sharing stories.

I served a new chicken Parmesan dish recommended and prepared by my butcher. It was succulent, a great treat we all savored. How wonderful to have this prepared for me and delivered hot to the door. My famous chicken curry takes several days for the flavors to blend—time I didn't have. Rather than not spending time with friends who had traveled great distances to be at the art opening, I simplified. After a month of traveling, we were happy to welcome friends in our home. It was a relaxed, joyful evening.

Keep your strong sense of purpose in mind. Strive to avoid extremes in order to seek the highest good. Carry on an inner conversation with your conscience. Question: Is this good? Is this good for me? Is this good for others? Whenever you begin to feel tense or anxious, bring yourself back to awareness of your breath. Breathe consciously. When we feel stress, our breathing becomes tight and restricted. Try doing some deep breathing exercises. Let your exhalation be twice as long as your inhalation. Look at the second hand of your watch or a clock and deliberately try to synchronize your breathing with the clockwise movement. This will immediately slow down your breath. Try to breathe deeply for several minutes, until you inhale and exhale six times per sixty seconds. Say an affirmation or a mantra to yourself when you breathe in. As you exhale, let go of everything. Be empty and you will be full of positive energy.

Visualize yourself on a beach in Hawaii with the sun on your back. The fresh breezes caress you; you're about to go for a swim. The waves pound in and you feel one with the ocean. Breathe into the moment. Visualize that you are in a beautiful flower garden on a glorious sunny day. Look at one flower—a daffodil, a tulip, a rose, or a pansy—and really see the color and beauty. With deep breathing, you feel as though you're absorbed into the essence of the flower. Slow down your pace. Move with grace. Practice mindful walking where you are aware of every step you take. Take time to look and really see everything in your immediate surroundings. Temporarily don't be conscious of externals, concentrate on your self-awareness. Listen to a motivational, inspirational tape by a favorite guru or philosopher to help you connect to your essence. Make a pot of tea and sit quietly to read some affirmations. No mindful time is ever overwhelming.

Try not to overdo. Excess causes disorder and dis-ease, taking us away from our purpose. Whenever we become overextended, we lose our center where we feel content in the moment. Too much and too little are not polar opposites but are connected in the shape of a circle. Our wholeness comes when we bring everything into the center of life, when we try to maintain a harmonious balance in our thoughts and actions. Remember Dr. Suvi's wise advice to Aunt Betty: "Moderation in everything, Betty, even virtue."

✻

MODERATION LASTS.

SENECA

CHAPTER SEVEN

Spirit

You're at the Banquet

Why are we here? What are we going to do with our time alive? What do you believe is worthy of your time? I want to feast on life.

In 1986, my book *Living a Beautiful Life: 500 Ways to Add Elegance, Order, Beauty and Joy to Every Day of Your Life* about celebrations, ceremonies, and rituals, was published. I had started writing it more than a decade before because I discovered that 95 percent of our daily lives is spent doing ordinary repetitious acts while only 5 percent is lived in celebration. I first learned this shocking fact from my interior design clients who were continuously preparing for some future time when their house would be "finished." *Then* they would have friends over, *then* they would play music, arrange flowers, light candles and enjoy the moments of their time alive at home. But *then* never comes. My belief is that we can and should turn the ordinary into the extraordinary by creating little celebrations. Now is all we will ever be given. A house is or should be a continuous work in progress; it is the background for an evolving life to be lived fully and deeply in celebration every moment of every day.

The time to light the lights is now, when we have eyes to see. The time to celebrate with our children is when they're still with us in the nest. The time to have friends over for a spontaneous supper is now while they're available, not "let's get together soon." Soon is never soon enough. The time to celebrate life *every* day has come. Today, look to this hour. There is no time to waste. Living a life without daily rituals, celebrations and ceremonies would be a glum and joyless existence.

Whether you're at home alone making a wonderful salad for lunch, or setting a pretty table for dinner with a friend or spouse, or packing a picnic basket to take to the beach with the grandchildren, the only time to celebrate is right this very minute in the midst of every detail and reality of your life.

No one can ever afford to put his or her time alive on hold. While we are alive with our body and senses, we're meant to love life more vigorously, more abundantly, by celebrating whatever we are doing. The simple acts of laying out your clothes, drawing a bath, bathing and dressing, can be as meaningful as a bride putting on her wedding dress when you awaken to the moment, present to all the nuances and subtleties of what you are experiencing.

I remember once when Peter and I went out to breakfast before going to the grocery store. We rarely go out to breakfast, so this was an unusual treat. Beyond shopping for food, we hadn't planned the day. At breakfast our server Victoria said, "Mr. Brown, you look spiffy. Are you going somewhere special?" Peter thanked her for the compliment: "No, I'm here," he said. "This is somewhere special." At the market, the woman bagging our groceries complimented Peter and me on our colorful clothes, "Are you going to a wedding or something?" "No, we're grocery shopping." Every occasion can be sweetened by creating a sense of fun and adventure when you realize that *all* time lived is important.

Time goes on eternally, but our time alive won't last long. I try to let my breath of life continuously remind me that there are only so many hours to celebrate, only so many more starry nights, so many full moons or new moons.

Cheer, toast, honor and love yourself, your life and your interconnection and interdependence on loved ones, your community and unknown others. Dance, sing, clap your hands. Give a standing ovation to a performer whether on Broadway or when your one-year-old daughter tries to take her first step. In the spirit of the banquet, I honor you.

LET US SUPPOSE THAT THERE ARE TWO SORTS OF EXISTENCES—ONE SEEN, THE OTHER UNSEEN ... THE SEEN IS THE CHANGING AND THE UNSEEN IS THE UNCHANGING.

SOCRATES

70

Trust Your True Self and Spirit

EVEN IF I ERR IN SAYING THAT THE SOUL IS ETERNAL, NEVERTHELESS I AM
HAPPY THAT I MADE THIS MISTAKE. AND WHILE I AM ALIVE, NOT A SINGLE
PERSON CAN TAKE AWAY THIS ASSURANCE, WHICH GIVES ME COMPLETE
CALMNESS AND GREAT SATISFACTION.

CICERO

You are a part of all there is, all there ever was, all that will ever be. Your Spirit-energy grows throughout your lifetime and must be kept charged and bright. You can't escape being a vital part of the experience of being alive. Even death doesn't make you disappear because your soul is and was and always will be nonmaterial, infinite.

You are an integral part of eternity. You are an eternal spirit temporarily existing in a physical body. You are so much more than you'll ever know or understand. None of us uses more than a small amount of our potential as human beings. Inside us is the intelligence of the universe waiting to be realized. There is so much more for us to bring forth. We need nothing we don't already possess. From birth to death our time alive is ours to act, to achieve, to create and acknowledge our role as co-creators.

When a friend went off to France for her junior year abroad, her father's parting words were, "Remember who you are." When we know and remember who we are, the universe speeds to guide us, encourage and sustain us. When we're being true to this highest knowledge and understanding of who we are, we grow in faith in our own self-reliance.

Depend on your higher Self. Everything is in place for you. Confidently know that you will not fail when you have firm reliance on your character and integrity. Patiently continue to grow, trusting your intuition that is your real guiding light. This inner knowing is instinctive. The truth will continuously be revealed to you without reason or outer knowledge. You possess this innate capacity of perception. Let this subtle, spontaneous awareness teach you who you essentially are.

Joseph Campbell understood our spirit's longings: "What we're really seeking is an experience of being alive, so that our life experiences on the purely physical plane will have resonance within our innermost being and reality, so that we can actually feel the rapture of being alive."

Trust your feelings, your energy. When you experience ecstasy, you will continue to trust your Self in the joy of being alive.

✤

I BELIEVE THAT MAN WILL NOT MERELY ENDURE: HE WILL PREVAIL.
HE IS IMMORTAL, NOT BECAUSE HE ALONE AMONG CREATURES HAS AN
INEXHAUSTIBLE VOICE, BUT BECAUSE HE HAS HIS SOUL, A SPIRIT CAPABLE OF
KINDNESS, COMPASSION, SACRIFICE AND ENDURANCE.

WILLIAM FAULKNER

71

Joy Accompanies a Courageous Life

COURAGE IS RIGHTLY ESTEEMED THE FIRST OF HUMAN QUALITIES...
IT IS THE QUALITY WHICH GUARANTEES ALL OTHERS.

WINSTON CHURCHILL

Once, while I was autographing a book after a talk in Nashville, Tennessee, a young mother told me that her six-year-old daughter had made her day: There was a bumper sticker on a car in front of theirs that read, "Life is good." The little girl said, "Mommy, that's wrong. Life is great."

Life is a dynamic experience. Our strength rises to meet our challenges. When we meet difficulties head-on with courage, joy comes to sweeten the atmosphere. Think back on the most challenging circumstances you have faced. With time, you come to understand that the difficulties that you overcome and meet bravely make you stronger. Many studies indicate that this is true.

We have a Unitarian minister friend in New York City who told us about a woman in his parish who was a chronic complainer. Every Sunday after the service she'd wait in line, usually wanting to be at the end so she could unravel her litany of complaints. "Oh, why is my husband an alcoholic? Why is my son on drugs? Why me?" One Sunday when she came again to the minister with more complaints, he turned to her in frustration and said under his breath, "Why not?"

Instead of asking "why me," look at each situation objectively. Ask yourself, "What can I learn from this? How can I deepen my understanding?"

When circumstances are beyond our control, we must accept reality coura-geously. One reality is that complaining too often increases the pain.

When we come to the end of our rope, something happens: we discover depths in us we never knew were there. We experience a fresh beginning. When we're able to overcome difficult situations, even catastrophic circum-stances, we build confidence that we'll never be completely overwhelmed.

Know now that you have the inborn strength to meet painful situations. Sad events happen to all of us; we are not alone in this human family, but con-nected. Even though you may feel alone, that no one else could possibly feel your sadness, other people not only have experienced similar situations, but, in many cases, worse. There are always people worse off than you are.

Christopher Reeve was a symbol of superhuman, raw courage. He per-sonified inspiration after a riding accident in 1995 left him paralyzed from the neck down. We ask ourselves, how does someone summon such courage? Perhaps Christopher Reeve didn't know he had it, but he refused to be crushed, providing a formula for bearing up as optimistically as possible under the force of a terrible blow. Refuse to accept others' reality. Never stop push-ing. Dream big, even the impossible.

John F. Kennedy's definition of courage holds true for Reeve: "every per-son must decide on it for himself and draw it from within." Reeve is a hero whose personal courage in dealing with his paralysis transcended his fine act-ing career and his exceptional leadership in many great causes. He believed that, "you have to stand up for yourself—even if you are sitting in a wheel-chair." He felt fortunate to have a loving family that "helps stand you in good stead in case something horrible happens." He left a legacy of joy during his time alive, struggling with rare bravery.

Joy is yours when you are courageous.

✻

THE OCCASION IS PILED HIGH WITH DIFFICULTY,
AND WE MUST RISE WITH THE OCCASION.

ABRAHAM LINCOLN

72

Refresh Your Inner Life Daily

CONTEMPLATION IS THE HIGHEST FORM OF ACTIVITY.

ARISTOTLE

*E*ver since I can remember, I've loved to be alone in my private world. I remember being four years old, hiding in a hayloft in the red barn behind our farm in Weston, Massachusetts. All of us have a need to escape into our inner life where we silently contemplate and observe.

In solitude we can concentrate on beauty, not the conflicts of our day-to-day lives. Here, we can avoid external unpleasantness, answering to our own conscience. Whenever we are alone and still, we enter the house of our soul. This innermost essence of our individual life needs to be nurtured *every* day.

Life on earth is lived from the inside out. In our time alive we must make a commitment to pay attention to the growth of our soul's illumination. We are alone in this world even though it is crowded with people and continuous activities. Our thoughts, longings and inner knowing will never be entirely understood by others. This part of us is not meant to be shared.

In solitude, paradoxically, we shatter our loneliness. Here, quietly, we enter into our intimate, eternal oneness with all there is. We can awaken within to the expansiveness of the universe. We come to understand that wisdom goes beyond all knowledge.

When we nourish our inner world, we let go of religious dogma, politics, and all the thousands of ways of separating us from our Self. Free from outside influences, we open ourselves wide to receive more of the mystery. The physical world is not the whole of who and what we are. All of us have inner work to do.

Take particularly good care of your whole Self. Physically, emotionally and mentally, you want to flower. Your inner life is paramount to everything you feel and do. Without a healthy inner life, you will feel lost. Spend sacred time alone each day. Read affirmations, poetry and good literature. Experiment until you establish a habitual routine to provide time and space for your inner growth. Remove yourself completely from the responsibilities, demands and role-playing of spouse, parent, teacher, boss, relative—let the silence calm your mind. In solitude we are no longer fragmented, but whole and complete. Whether we read sacred texts or quietly meditate, pray, walk, sing or dance, in silence we seek to unite body and soul.

Our soul awaits our undivided attention *every* day. When we put in the time, when we listen and are receptive to our essential nature, we form an integration of our inner essence and our outer actions. The more rigorous our unseen inner-work, the more our outer activities will be dynamic expressions of our whole Self. Faithfully listen to the truth inside your Self.

❀

ORIGINAL THOUGHT IS THE PRODUCT
NOT OF THE BRAIN BUT OF THE FULL SELF.

ROBERT GRUDIN

73

You Can Find Inner Peace, Even in a Storm

LEARN TO WISH THAT EVERYTHING SHOULD COME
TO PASS EXACTLY AS IT DOES.

EPICTETUS

*W*hen we learn to live from our center, we know that all inner peace comes from inside our hearts and souls. We can always go there. Remember, storms are in the circumference of our life. We can go inside and shut the door.

We will continuously be challenged as we move through our adventurous life's journey. Often we have unrelenting demands on our time and continuous drains on our resources. Other people's expectations and needs can cause stress, strain, worry and confusion. In stormy times we can become shipwrecked if we're not careful to stay centered, connected to our Self, our soul.

If I weren't in the habit of going inward I'm convinced I'd feel frazzled most of the time because I choose to live an extremely active life. Now that our daughter Brooke is married, we've turned her bedroom into an art gallery. There is no furniture in the middle of this large space, making it ideal for meditation. I light a candle; I ring a bell to remind me to be mindful; I sit on my yoga mat in lotus position, hands in prayer pressed toward my heart. Here, alone, I turn inward. I lose my self-consciousness. I chant "om" on a deep exhalation. I feel the vibration in my ears, throat, brain and limbs—my whole being. Do this exercise several times and see how it elevates your spirit.

Away from my home office, getting centered, concentrating on breathing deepiy, I sit and take time to nurture my soul. Even if I only do this for four or five minutes, I emerge feeling refreshed. By regularly going inward, I'm able to feel exhilaration where others may feel exhaustion.

Another useful exercise I recommend: Lie down on a mat or rug on the floor. Stretch yourself so you are elongated. Shake out your hands and feet; really move your fingers and toes. Wriggle your shoulders and neck. Close your eyes. Shed all your worries and all fears. Feel your body and your breath. Within three minutes you will feel more balanced. Open your eyes, roll over to your right side and slowly sit up. Repeat your mantra. It could be "love my time alive."

Our inner resources are our compasses, determining the direction of our lives. The innermost part of us is calm. Whenever you find your mind spinning out of control, stop. Ask yourself if you are contributing to the storm. Sometimes if I feel agitated I know I am to blame for cutting back on my contemplative time.

There will be turbulent times, attacks against us, even rage. But when we're aware of our own thoughts and emotions, we're able to go to the center of our being and there we will find the peace we are seeking.

Try not to judge situations or people. Be personally responsible for your Self. Do whatever is necessary not to encourage storms or create them. Keep drawing yourself back inward to your center. With your balance and perspective, the center will hold. You will find inner peace in all circumstances.

Accept life's challenges and overcome difficulties, knowing they are all a part of this thrilling adventure of life right here, right now.

✳

OH, ONLY TO LIVE, LIVE, LIVE! LIVE UNDER
ANY CIRCUMSTANCES—ONLY TO LIVE!

DOSTOYEVSKY

74

Try Not to Act Your Age

REMEMBER THAT YOU ARE NOT MORTAL; ONLY YOUR BODY IS MORTAL.
WHAT IS ALIVE IS NOT YOUR BODY BUT THE SPIRIT LIVING IN YOUR BODY.
AN UNSEEN FORCE GUIDES YOUR BODY, JUST AS AN UNSEEN FORCE GUIDES
THE WORLD.

CICERO

Our Spirit-energy is ageless. We can and should live with a flourish to the end of our time. When we're in the swing, in the groove, feeling the vitalizing flow of Spirit, we remain young at heart. Keep alive the spirit of wonder. Your Spirit is the teacher of truth. We age, become ill and die earlier when we restrict our Spirit's freedom.

Scientists are now researching the benefits of humor, laughter and playfulness on our health. When we sing, we build our immune system. We become old when we are no longer having fun, when we don't put our full intensity into whatever we're doing.

When I was on *Oprah*, a producer asked an anthropologist and me to skip toward a house where they were filming. Cut! The serious man had neglected his Spirit for so many years that he'd forgotten how to skip. When was the last time you leapt for joy?

A harried young mother of two, expecting her third child, confided in me recently that she never plays with her children. She's too busy organizing their lives and watching out for their safety. What a loss for all of them. At every age we can keep our Spirit-energy vitally alive when we move our bodies and engage our minds in fun activities. Ride on the carousel. Go down the slide. Swing. Jump on the trampoline. Hop around in the moon bounce. Take a dance class. Let your Spirit move you. Pretend you're going on a trip around the world. Where would you go? Who would you bring along? What would you do? What foods would you eat? Let your intellectual imagination soar. Visualize your spring garden and make some sketches. Design your dream house. Fantasize. Write a groovy children's book to make your grandchildren giggle. Continue to make visualization a fun habit. Make believe and there you are! Engage in as many fun, happy experiences as you can imagine. Life is a dance, not a spectator sport. Your Spirit is ageless and knows no bounds.

Don't allow anyone or anything to clip your wings. Try not to act your age or you will accelerate the aging process. Your cells are healthiest and happiest when your Spirit soars. Your Spirit is powerful, giving you the strength and vitality to do great things. Keep your Spirit-energy alive and young.

❋

SOME LEARN TOO LATE OR NOT AT ALL
THE LAST GREAT LESSON OF LIFE: SPIRITUAL QUALITIES ATTEND
THE SOUL MORE THAN FIXATION ON MATERIAL EXCESS.

PETER MEGARGEE BROWN

75

Your True Essence Is Love

LOVE IS A MEDICINE FOR THE SICKNESS OF THE WORLD;
A PRESCRIPTION OFTEN GIVEN, TOO RARELY TAKEN.

LOVE CURES PEOPLE—BOTH THE ONES WHO GIVE IT AND
THE ONES WHO RECEIVE IT.

WILLIAM C. MENNINGER, M.D.

*L*ove is the most powerful energy of all. We can choose love. We can cultivate love. We can be in love in all aspects of our lives, in all forms. Wherever there is love, there is life. Love never dies. Love is the purest, most eternal, everlasting essence of our soul. Our love will heal, restore, refresh and transcend us and the lives we touch.

In my book, *Living in Love*, I wrote about being in love with people, places and things. The more we love, the more we live, the greater our sense of purpose, the richer our life-satisfaction. Our happiness and well-being, our inner wealth, directly benefit from our capacity to love.

We were not all brought up to encourage loving of our Self. We were raised to love and serve others. But when we honor ourselves, when we value the time and effort that we take to know and love ourselves, then we're in a position to better love and be more useful to others.

What's interesting about this compelling force of love within us is that genuine love transcends our ego, our narrow self-interests. When we love ourselves, we're free to love others. The love in our hearts connects to the love in someone else's soul.

When we have a deep, tender, ineffable feeling of affection toward another person, this energy creates a sense of underlying oneness—not just with an individual, but with all of creation. We become open, receptive to the absolute, profound divine force of unconditional love.

Think of those people you feel strong attachment toward, who you greatly enjoy and love. Take a few minutes to write down their names. Do you have a dog or cat or bird as a pet that you dearly love? Do you love your house? Identify all the different forms of your loves. Are you attached to the spirit of a place where you enjoy going on vacation? What are some of the objects you most treasure in your home? I love the paintings we collect by our friend Roger Mühl. I love the photographs of our children and grandchildren that help keep wonderful memories alive.

Do you love your chosen work? Whatever you do, when you act in a loving consciousness, you increase your life-force, your vital energy. When we fill our life with love, we help people to feel this love force in their own heart. When we love, we don't judge. We accept. We're kind. We're understanding. Love is the sunshine, the smile, the honey of life. Love sweetens sadness, and makes us feel completely alive to what is deepest in our human heart.

Love life. Live in love in all relationships. Love unifies us. Embrace all that is true, beautiful and good in loving, tender ways. Spread your loving energy as far as your imagination goes. We're born to love. Where there is great love, we are transformed. We're lifted up.

In your remaining time alive, recognize your true essence is love. Live each moment in this consciousness. My mantra is "Love & Live Happy." Focus on all that you love—people, places, animals, scenery, mountains, gardens, villages, towns, cities, islands, beaches, lakes, oceans and dazzling skies. Open your heart wide to all that you recognize as beautiful. When you live in the energy of pure love, you are fulfilling your destiny. You are one with all there is. Love is all. This force lives in all things. Love is not just an emotion. Love is the most powerful force within you.

❊

LOVE IS NOT A PASSIVE STATE. IT IS AN ACTIVE FORCE. IT IS THE FORCE OF THE SOUL.

EVENTUALLY YOU WILL COME TO UNDERSTAND
THAT LOVE HEALS EVERYTHING, AND LOVE IS ALL THERE IS.

GARY ZUKAV

76

Appreciate the Mysteries of Grace

THE WINDS OF GRACE BLOW ALL THE TIME. ALL WE NEED
TO DO IS SET OUR SAILS

SRI RAMAKRISHNA

*W*hether we're always aware of it or not, grace is unmerited assistance that appears at just the right time and place. This divine force is supremely good. With the right attitude and perspective, we can experience grace in all things. We can't find it by seeking; we appreciate and accept grace when we feel it.

The peak experience just appears out of the blue. The ecstatic moment comes to greet us. There is no pain or confusion, no problems or contradiction. Grace tickles us with a divine presence. One of my favorite Rumi poems is "Zero Circle":

✻ Be helpless, dumbfounded,
Unable to say yes or no.
Then a stretcher will come from grace
to gather us up.

as translated by Coleman Barks ✻

The great gift of grace is that it is freely bestowed. Grace is invisible and untouchable. Grace comes to *us*, surrounds us and envelops us. Grace is ineffable, eluding our understanding. Instead of trying to understand the mystery, we may come to see we are part of it. We can choose to be open and receptive to the gift of grace, rather than trying to comprehend it. Instead of saying you know or don't know, you can open yourself to sense what is there. No amount of reading about grace creates the grace-filled experience. Whether you are good or bad, you are the embodiment of grace. You don't have to be worthy. Breathe it in.

Unlike nature, grace is always good, waiting to be seen and felt. Grace is everywhere, in every place, in every person. Grace is not scientific. You can't describe it, you can't prove it, you can't examine it or explain it to anyone's satisfaction. We receive grace through every experience in life. Grace is out there, around us and inside us. Accept its paradoxes. If we could solve the mystery of grace it would not be as powerful. Life, too, *is* paradoxical. We live this tension. Life is made up of pain and pleasure. We don't ask for sorrow, but often the people who have experienced a great deal of pain are the ones who make the most of their lives. When we accept the paradoxical realities of life, we deepen and are strengthened.

There are lots of ambiguities in life. You'll never figure everything out. Sages give us paradoxical messages—"empty and be full," "the last shall be first," "the way to do is to be." As human beings we can embrace this amazing range of eternal truths. The ultimate truth could be to accept grace unconditionally. For a person to be fully alive in time, to have a sense of the phenomenon of grace can be a helpful factor in making a complete life. It would be a shame to have lived your life and not to have accepted this great gift given to us. No matter what your beliefs, don't miss the universal heartbeat of grace. No one is excluded.

To show our appreciation for this powerful mysterious blessing, "all we need to do is set our sails." Feel the mighty force of the winds of grace. There are times when we're able to exchange thoughts and information through divine love and protection through prayer. Grace provides an effortless ease that creates intimacy and happiness. This goes far beyond words.

Emerson believed prayer is seeing life from the highest point of view. I believe that prayer is our sublime communication with everyone and everything we love—and it encourages the mystery of grace.

The words of the famous hymn come to mind—indeed, grace is amazing.

✿

AMAZING GRACE! HOW SWEET THE SOUND
THAT SAVED A WRETCH LIKE ME!
I ONCE WAS LOST, BUT NOW AM FOUND;
WAS BLIND, BUT NOW I SEE.

'TWAS GRACE THAT TAUGHT MY HEART TO FEAR,
AND GRACE MY FEARS RELIEVED;
HOW PRECIOUS DID THAT GRACE APPEAR
THE HOUR I FIRST BELIEVED.

THROUGH MANY DANGERS, TOILS AND SNARES,
I HAVE ALREADY COME;
'TIS GRACE HATH BROUGHT ME SAFE THUS FAR,
AND GRACE WILL LEAD ME HOME.

77

Accept Your Divine Potential as Your Birthright

*E*ver since I traveled around the world in 1959, I've been fascinated by world religions and Eastern philosophy. I read and study about the divine Spirit, the soul, mysticism and metaphysics. Daily I do my spiritual homework, beginning and ending in meditation. My daily discipline keeps me focused as I plunge into the depth of the mystery and miracle of being alive.

Words are completely inadequate to describe the miraculous. Literal-minded scientists want proof of what lies beyond physical existence. I believe that the largest part of us is intangible, invisible, untouchable Spirit-energy. We are human and we are divine. The spiritual forces within are more powerful than material forces. How do we reconcile nature and Spirit?

When we discover the divine in our own self, we begin to see that divinities are everywhere, waiting to be discovered. We come to understand that everything alive is supremely good in potential. We see with an inner eye the magnificence of the sacred everywhere. We're in awe. We have a transcendent reverence for being alive. We are the miraculous, the superhuman. Nature is divine in having nurtured us. Think of the miracle, the divine intelligence, of one human body and soul becoming alive and being born in forty weeks.

Creation, creator, you and me. All things are in divinity. We become fully alive when we accept our divine potential. This is our birthright. This is our true nature, our value.

Our divine potential is inexhaustible. We can spend the rest of our lives trying to transcend to higher states of consciousness and, at the end of our time alive, will not have reached all of our divine potential. Whatever we accomplish, all that we create on earth has to be done here and now. I'm humbled to realize how valuable our time is to use our capacity to bring something of ourselves into actuality.

Every morning I literally want to wake up, find out who I really am, and live the greatest hours of truth I can while the time is available. Our consciousness evolves from low levels of awareness to becoming highly spiritually developed. Think of the examples of human beings you admire throughout history who worked to wisely and mindfully use their full divine powers.

We can come to know who we are by contacting this inner space where we are connected to the collective universal intelligence. All there ever was, all there ever will be, is available to us within. The more light we feel, the more radiant our inner sun, the more peace, creativity, confidence and faith we have as we try to use our divine powers well.

We're born innocent, but not wise. We evolve when we're committed to our inner work; when we use our time to become full, conscious of our innate Spirit-energy, our divine potential. Accept this gift. There is so much more to who we are than what meets the eye. We must use our lifetime to bring out more from this great resource. We are miraculous in our human ability to perfect our divine potential.

✸

ONLY WHEN THIS EVOLVING CONSCIOUSNESS CAN GROW
INTO ITS OWN FULL DIVINE POWER WILL WE DIRECTLY KNOW
OURSELVES AND THE WORLD.

SRI AUROBINDO

78

Contemplate Life from the Highest Point of View

THERE COMES A TIME WHEN THE MIND TAKES A HIGHER PLANE
OF KNOWLEDGE BUT CAN NEVER PROVE HOW IT GOT THERE.

ALBERT EINSTEIN

*W*hen we give our all to everything we choose to do, we rise above the ordinary, giving new inspiration to our higher nature. There is so much good we can do to make the world a better place for abundant living. Aim high. Continue to be a blessing.

Open doors and windows to let in more light. Let your new thoughts, your awareness and consciousness elevate you to a fresh commitment to deepen your journey. Every step you climb leads you higher and higher to greater truth, to knowing your central place in the world.

Your ideal self is inside you. Give birth to your innate greatness. Confidently move in the direction of your dreams. There is so much more in you, so much more to life than you now envision, so much you can bring into being.

When we get in tune with our divine spirit, we transcend our time alive to understand our oneness with all that is. The world is inside us. All the light, love, goodness and creativity are within us. Our task and responsibility is to find the truth in our soul.

The outside world is as much a part of you as your inner world. Embrace each day as a great opportunity to thrive. Look for the good that is everywhere. Focus on all that is constructive. Let your inner light shine on your immediate surroundings.

Your power is right where you are now. Value your experience here and now. The creator is the creation. Know your oneness, your life-sustaining love energy. Life *is* a mystery. We are the mystery. Have as much of this rich living experience as you can. Relish the wonder of it all. Accept nature as it is and acknowledge your transcendent nature as you evolve. Take time to listen to the creative process. The whole support of the universe is available to you and me right where we are. You and I are divinely guided and directed.

Contemplate your life as a masterpiece. Let your creative intentions be pure and loving. Continue to elevate your thoughts to the highest conscious levels where you feel the mystery beautifully expressing itself through you.

❀

EVERY MAN WHO RISES ABOVE THE COMMON LEVEL HAS RECEIVED
TWO EDUCATIONS: THE FIRST FROM HIS TEACHERS; THE SECOND,
MORE PERSONAL AND IMPORTANT, FROM HIMSELF.

EDWARD GIBBON

79

Grow in Gratitude

GRATITUDE IS NOT ONLY THE GREATEST OF VIRTUES,
BUT THE PARENT OF ALL THE OTHERS.

CICERO

*W*hen I think of gratitude, I tend to define it as relationship with people. There are angels known and unknown who play significant roles in the quality and happiness of our lives.

I don't think any of us really knows how much we mean to each other. One of the most meaningful experiences for us is to be able to thank these wonderful souls for their contribution to our lives. Take a moment to identify some of these people who have touched you. Write their names down, leaving a space for you to jot down a brief description of their assistance to your growth.

There is no self-made person. We all have people who appear in our lives to inspire us, guide us, and encourage our creativity, our happiness, and our success. I believe that these people don't appear by coincidence. I grow more deeply grateful when I acknowledge the significance of so many caring people who have encouraged the growth and direction of my path.

At the impressionable age of fifteen I met and became close to an eccentric Englishwoman, Phyl Gardner, who taught art at a boarding school I attended in Massachusetts. Phyl and her husband, Jimmy, never had their own children, so their favorite students became their family. Artist Phyl and architect Jimmy encouraged me to pursue a career as a designer.

Many people who are important to us are no longer alive. But many are alive and well and would be touched to hear from us. It's time to remember and acknowledge the many souls who have shown you the light. Life is short. The best and only time to enhance our sense of gratitude is now. Whether you make a phone call, write a letter, send a small gift or arrange for a visit, both you and this significant other person in your life will be uplifted in the exchange. If people you love have died, you can connect with their children, telling them stories they will cherish, becoming friends with them as well.

I'm certain your list is long. Continue to lift these people up on angels' wings. Reinforce the goodness of others. Reward someone who has provided you with something supremely good.

✳

APPRECIATION IS A WONDERFUL THING; IT MAKES WHAT IS
EXCELLENT IN OTHERS BELONG TO US AS WELL.

VOLTAIRE

80

Tomorrow You Will Begin Again

THE SUN HAS CLIMBED THE HILL, THE DAY IS ON THE
DOWNWARD SLOPE . . . MY SOUL IS HEAVY WITH SUNSHINE,
AND STEEPED WITH STRENGTH . . . IT IS THE MOMENT OF FULNESS,
AND THE TOP OF THE MORNING.

D.H. LAWRENCE

*W*hen our day makes our soul "heavy with sunshine," when we can say that "this is the best day, tomorrow will be better," we are fully enjoying our lives. The sun will rise to renew us. Everything good we do today is carried with us as we begin again tomorrow.

When I give talks I like to remind those in attendance that we will never awaken to tomorrow. Each sunrise is a fresh new today, the beginning of whatever you choose to do with your gift of time.

Each dawn we awaken to a new opportunity to refresh ourselves completely. As we rise, we make up our mind to make the best use of our time this new day. What good things do you choose to accomplish? Today, begin while the sun is up and out. Once you've started, the soul "becomes steeped with strength." Most things are better in the morning when you are refreshed by a good night's sleep.

Every morning I tell myself and then tell Peter, "This is going to be the best day of our lives—so far." When we're alive, there's hope. Nothing is more important than to cherish this day. I smile when I remember the motto for an Italian preschool: *Niente senza gioia* (*Nothing without joy*).

When we wake up in the morning we can choose to think the thoughts that are going to be the most positive and that will produce the greatest good. This moment is ours to become better, more open, more loving, more alive.

As we take our first steps toward creating an ideal day, in order to make the world a better place, we have to make a sweet paradise right here, right now. Let your footprints sprout colorful flowers. Let the sunlight echo your soul's light.

This is your day. Embrace each moment with all your heart. Feel the blessing of your time alive to begin again, to live the great mystery.

❋

HOPE IS THE THING WITH FEATHERS
THAT PERCHES IN THE SOUL,
AND SINGS THE TUNE WITHOUT THE WORDS,
AND NEVER STOPS AT ALL.

EMILY DICKINSON